W9-ALV-586

SHOWS ABOUT NOTHING

SHOWS ABOUT NOTHING

Nihilism in Popular Culture
from The Exorcist *to* Seinfeld

THOMAS S. HIBBS

SPENCE PUBLISHING COMPANY • DALLAS

1999

Copyright © 1999 by Thomas S. Hibbs
First hardcover impression December 1999
First paperback impression December 2000

Published in the United States by
Spence Publishing Company
111 Cole Street
Dallas, Texas 75207

Library of Congress Cataloging-in-Publication Data
for the Hardcover Edition

Hibbs, Thomas S.
    Shows about nothing : nihilism in popular culture from the
Exorcist to Seinfeld / Thomas S. Hibbs
        p. cm.
    Includes bibliographical references and index.
    ISBN 1-890626-17-1
    1. Nihilism (Philosophy) in motion pictures.   2. Nihilism
(Philosophy) on television.   3. Evil in motion pictures.   I. Title.
PN1995.9.N55H53   1999
791.43'684—dc21   99-36845

ISBN 1-890626-35-x (pbk.)

Printed in the United States of America

For

Rev. Bill Parent

and

Tom Ponton

Contents

vii

Acknowledgments

I HAVE INCURRED a number of debts in the process of writing this book. The initial draft of the book was completed during a sabbatical granted by Boston College and further supported by a grant from the Lynde and Harry Bradley Foundation. On at least three occasions I have profited from the opportunity to present material from the book to students at Boston College. For their receptivity and questions I am grateful. Mitch Muncy and Tom Spence of Spence Publishing have been enthusiastic and helpful from the moment I first described the project to them. Along the way, numerous individuals generously agreed to read and comment on part or all of the manuscript. Deserving of special mention are Brian Braman, Henry Brinton, Mike Dubik, Stanley Hauerwas, Stacey Hibbs, William Hibbs, John O'Callaghan, Mark O'Connor, Bill Parent, Tom Ponton, and Kelcey Wilson.

Other than my wife, Stacey, and my father, William, both of whom are obliged to put up with me and at least to humor my reflections on philosophy and popular culture, Bill Parent and Tom Ponton are perhaps most responsible for fostering my addiction to popular culture. Tom Ponton has been a friend since our days together as students at DeMatha High School, where he is now director of development. Bill Parent, now a priest for the Archdiocese of Washington, D.C., has been a friend for nearly as long. To them I dedicate whatever there is here of a book.

SHOWS ABOUT NOTHING

Beyond Good and Evil

IN RECENT YEARS, America has been stunned by a series of brutal murders perpetrated by children. Americans have of course been terrorized by murderers before. Serial killers, from Manson and Berkowitz to Ramirez and Dahmer, have often held the national imagination captive, and their wacky theories have become as notorious as the heinous acts they committed. The most notable is certainly Manson's "helter skelter" theory of the collapse of America. Berkowitz claimed he was obeying the commands of Satan, who spoke to him through the incessant howling of his neighbor's dog, Sam. After he was apprehended, Ramirez taunted citizens, the media, and the justice system with the Nietzschean line, "I'm beyond you. I'm beyond good and evil."

These serial killers were bizarre, lonely adults, denizens of cities where, in the 1970s and 1980s, Americans had almost become accustomed to the constant threat of violence. The unease caused by the child murderers, all of whom were

3

caught soon after they committed their crimes, has been of a somewhat different sort. Schoolyards and gymnasia, once considered safe havens, have been suddenly transformed into shooting galleries. From Paducah, Kentucky, and Jonesboro, Arkansas, to Pearl, Mississippi, Springfield, Oregon, and Littleton, Colorado, towns known for nothing other than their decent, law-abiding citizens have produced children capable of demonic deeds. Aside from the settings and multiple victims, another common feature of these killings has been the influence on the perpetrators of films such as *Natural Born Killers* and *Basketball Diaries*, of fantasy video games, and of the nihilistic lyrics of Marilyn Manson.[1] Some of these precocious children even claimed to have been reading Nietzsche. Whatever one makes of the causal relationship between the endemic violence of our popular culture and the behavior of those immersed in it, this much is clear: the universal availability of popular culture—through videos, television, radio, and the internet—means that no one can escape its influence.

Michael Medved, one of our most informed and eloquent critics of contemporary mores, notes that we have no other culture than popular culture, and popular culture is Hollywood, especially television, culture. In *Hollywood vs. America: Popular Culture and the War on Traditional Values*,[2] Medved details Hollywood's strong amoralist bent and argues that the entertainment industry is hostile to mainstream American values. There is little doubt that Hollywood's nihilism has the effect of coarsening our public life, desensitizing us to violence, and making us generally more cynical.[3] Immersion in its powerful images could be considered a morally neutral form of entertainment only by someone already thoroughly jaded. In its celebration of the grotesque artistry of destruction, of evil for its own sake, and of untutored, adolescent self-expression, Hollywood promotes a debased, Nietzschean culture—the side of Nietzsche that values unrestrained creativity.

It does not follow from Hollywood's nihilism, however, that the primary target of the entertainment industry is the traditional values espoused by Republicans or the Christian Coalition. Such hostility is incidental, for nihilism cuts much more deeply: it attacks the very foundations of modern politics, whose assumptions the Left and Right share. Nihilism calls into question democratic ideals such as individual rights and human dignity, the politics of equality and consensus, the pursuit of happiness, the possibility of progress, even modern science and medicine. These ideals supply the framework for the good life and the principles for our discernment of good and evil. If they are exposed as bankrupt, to move beyond good and evil, to attempt to transcend moral conventions, can be seen as liberating, a perverse affirmation of life and freedom in opposition to a degrading moral system. The pursuit of evil, then, can have a certain grandeur to it—or at least seem cool and hip. On this point, there is a striking convergence between the aesthetics of our popular culture and the pursuit of evil by serial killers and child murderers.

It is precisely this convergence that leads critics of Hollywood to rail against its corrupt value system. But these critics would do well to ponder the following questions: Why does our democratic culture breed demonic characters? And why are Americans so captivated by these figures of rebellion, real or fictional? Indeed, the American fascination with crime and criminality remains high even as there has been a remarkable decline in serious crime in most large cities. Furthermore, nihilistic premises pervade our popular culture, not just through horror films and violent movies-of-the-week, but through the most successful sitcoms of the last decade, *The Simpsons* and *Seinfeld*. Is there perhaps some link between American democracy and nihilism? Can our contemporary popular culture be seen as drawing out the natural consequences of certain strains of liberal individualism? These are precisely the questions I explore. That thinkers as diverse and profound as Friedrich Nietzsche, Alexis de Tocqueville, T. S. Eliot, and Hannah Arendt have detected a subtle link between nihilism and certain forms of democratic liberalism lends credibility to affirmative answers.

Although this book is more about popular culture than it is about philosophy, I spend some time, especially in the first chapter, examining philosophical accounts of nihilism, which Nietzsche describes as the moral state in which the highest values devalue themselves, human aspiration shrinks, and the great questions and elevating quests of previous ages no longer have any resonance in the human soul. Having laid this foundation, I will turn to film and television, focusing on the most famous and influential portrayals of evil and on the mainstream popularity of nihilistic comedies. Along the way, I also point out the most creative attempts to avert or overcome nihilism.

This book, then, is a work of applied philosophy that will attempt to shed light on both popular culture and nihilism. On the side of popular culture, if I am right about the way it confirms the insights of certain philosophers about the link between democratic liberalism and nihilism, any critique of our popular culture that ignores the complex historical and political forces that have shaped it is apt to be superficial and leave us blind to the sources and lines of battle in the so-called "culture war." On the side of philosophy, we learn that nihilism is not, as many suppose, an era of chaos and disorder. Instead, it involves a simplification of human nature, a reduction of its complexity and range, and an abridgment of its aspirations. The nuanced richness of human life gives way to a mechanistic and predictable pattern of behavior, embodied in a limited set of fairly inflexible narrative structures. The dominant narrative structure is cyclical, expressing a sense of entrapment and unveiling progress and development as illusory. From the revenge plots of the movies-of-the-week, to the conspiratorial artistry of the *X-Files*, to *Seinfeld*'s magisterial use of coincidence to undermine the aspirations of its main characters, we confront an implacable and inexorable force, a malevolent power that prevents not only moral transformation and understanding, but even escape.

Doubts about the meaning of life and suggestions that it may ultimately be pointless are not peculiar to our era; indeed, the threat of nihilism seems to be coextensive with human life. It was certainly taken seriously in ancient Greek tragedy and even in the Jewish and Christian Scriptures. Tragedies focus on noble but less than perfect individuals whose flaws conspire with adverse circumstances to bring about their downfall. The nobility and complex humanity of the hero fosters an emotional connection between audience and character. The cathartic emotions of pity and fear that Aristotle associates with tragedy both presuppose and give expression to the sympathetic link. Tragedy tempers all human aspiration—for communication, love, and understanding, as well as power and honor. On the surface, its foremost counsel is one of moderation, but it never treats properly human aspirations as absurd or entirely misguided.

Tragedy locates the grandeur of human life in the gap between aspiration and achievement.

By contrast, comedies focus on ordinary people who face a series of trials, dilemmas, or difficulties in an attempt to achieve what they want. Whereas the evil in a tragedy is fully revealed only at the peak of the drama, the encounter with evil in comedy occurs early. Instead of chance conspiring to bring about a disproportionately harmful outcome, it orchestrates a benevolent conclusion which leads the main characters to a destiny that exceeds their merits and hopes. While the ending of a tragedy typically accentuates the isolation of the main character, comedies culminate in reconciliation and union: the stage of Shakespeare's tragedies is often strewn with corpses, while the final scene of his comedies is usually a wedding.

Once nihilism becomes a pervasive cultural assumption, however, neither classical tragedy nor classical comedy is possible, for nihilism wreaks havoc upon these genres. The conflict between the hero who stands beyond good and evil and the constricting, if timid, mores of conventional society, may contain residual elements of tragedy. But if nothing positive emerges from nihilistic rebellion, the ennobling vision of classical tragedy vanishes. The dramatic confluence of nihilism and evil therefore tends toward comedy, but this brand of comedy shares almost nothing with classical comedy. Just as in classical tragedy, in classical comedy the audience sympathizes with the characters. The harm done in classical comedy is only apparent or is seen to have a benign, instructive purpose, and our desire that things turn out well is never thwarted. By contrast, most contemporary sitcoms specialize in detached, ironic humor that portrays genuine suffering as funny. *The Simpsons,* for example, treats the arbitrary infliction of misery as a source of amusement, though even *The Simpsons* alternates between mocking cruelty and sentimental, familial embraces. *Seinfeld*, on the other hand, drops the sentimentality. Its writers abide by two commandments: no hugs, no learning.

A point of clarification is in order concerning the convergence of the speculations of philosophers and the artistic ethos of contemporary Hollywood. Except where there is explicit evidence, I do not claim that those behind the films and television shows I will examine are aware of, or in any way explicitly subscribe to, certain philosophical theses. And none of these productions embodies anything like a theory of nihilism: their allusive framework is entirely exhausted by the evanescent images of popular culture itself, and reference to great texts, or even classic films, is improbable. Yet the absence of any explicit influence of philosophical nihilism on popular culture highlights the significance of the unintended convergence. That such themes should nonetheless come to dominate our popular culture indicates that they are readily available within the culture itself and need not be imported from foreign philosophies.

The thesis of the book is that our popular culture is in large part informed by a demonic anti-providence. This is not devil worship but rather a vision of the American dream turned nightmare, a vision of America as a place where our pursuit of happiness is endlessly frustrated by powers beyond our control. We thus have reason to doubt that there is such a thing as the naked public square bemoaned by religious conservatives and celebrated by secular liberals. Such a claim is apt to prove disconcerting to both the right and the left, but it is a claim with which we must reckon and from which we can learn much.

I

Nihilism, American Style

IN THE 1991 FILM *Cape Fear*, the evil protagonist, played by Robert DeNiro, takes breaks from terrorizing, mutilating, biting, blinding, and raping the locals to visit the library and read *Thus Spake Zarathustra* by Friedrich Nietzsche, the nineteenth-century German philosopher best known for announcing the death of God. *Cape Fear*, directed by one of Hollywood's premier directors, Martin Scorsese, makes frequent reference to the philosophy of Nietzsche. Fragments of Nietzsche's thought now permeate our popular culture. Indeed, Harvey C. Mansfield calls Nietzsche the philosopher of our times.

Both scholars and laymen see Nietzsche as the philosopher of nihilism—the era, according to Nietzsche, of the ultimate degradation and degeneration of man. Francis Fukuyama caused a stir when he suggested, in *The End of History and the Last Man*,[1] that the nearly worldwide acceptance of democracy means we are now living in a post-revolutionary age, that humanity has no great battles left to fight, and hence that we have reached the end of history. Absent some clearly defined enemy or profound challenge, there is a danger that the tensions and springs of human greatness will dissipate, that human beings will become what Nietzsche called the "last men," who have a calm indifference to all elevated aspirations.

NIETZSCHE AND DEMOCRATIC NIHILISM

In *Thus Spake Zarathustra*, the eponymous hero predicts the coming of the last man: "Alas, the time of the most despicable man is coming, he that is no longer able to despise himself. Behold, I show you the last man. What is love? What is creation? What is longing? What is a star? Thus asks the last man and blinks. The earth has become small, and on it hops the last man who makes everything small."[2] The last man is timid, enervated, self-enclosed, and self-satisfied, an industrious economic animal who always finds it in his interest to go with the flow, to conform to the dictates of common opinion. Yet he does not regard this conformity and passivity as slavish because there is no one person to whom he submits. In following the majority, he does but follow his own will. Zarathustra expatiates: "No shepherd and one herd. Everybody wants the same, everybody is the same: whoever feels different goes voluntarily into a madhouse. . . . One has one's little pleasure for the day and one's little pleasure for the night: but one has a regard for health." When Zarathustra speaks these words to ordinary citizens, instead of being insulted by his description of their shallow and petty souls, they clamor, "turn us into these last men."

Nietzsche is virulently anti-democratic, for he believes that the politics and science of the Enlightenment preserve

what ought to perish and are at war with greatness and sin-
gularity. The imperative of the herd, he tells us, is that there
should "one day be nothing anymore to be afraid of."[3] The
herd's longing for a cessation of struggle, though, is an
"antibiological" pathology: "Life itself is a consequence of
war; society a means to war." Democratic morality is the
code of the slave, who finds existence so painful that he needs
morality and religion to make life worth living. But his morality is essentially one of utility; his religion one of pity.
Nietzsche scorns the modern, liberal notion of progress with
its goals of equality and the easing of all physical and psychic trials. He contrasts the slavish with the noble: "You
want . . . to abolish suffering. And we? It really seems that
we would rather have it higher and worse than ever. Well-
being as you understand it—that is no goal, that seems to us
an end, a state that soon makes man ridiculous and contemptible—that makes his destruction desirable." Only
through the "discipline of great suffering" does man, the "as
yet undetermined animal," develop.[4]

Not all conform to common opinion, however, especially
the opinion concerning the equality of all. In some there
remains the desire for excellence, for transcending the life
of the herd. The society of the last man is adept at satisfying nearly all desires for pleasure, but it cannot satiate, indeed it positively frustrates, the will to excel, to prove oneself
superior to others, and thereby to win recognition and admiration. The part of the soul that seeks excellence, which
Plato called the spirited part, displays itself in circumstances
of danger and risk and finds little room for exercise in the
competition with neighbors for the accumulation of better,
newer, and bigger consumer goods.

Spiritedness is distinct from the other passionate part of the soul, the erotic. Classically understood, *eros* is not reducible to the desire for bodily pleasure, even less to the gratification of the sexual appetite, but encompasses these desires within a longing for beauty and wholeness. By offering citizens an endless array of petty delights, consumer societies eviscerate *eros* and sap the human soul of its elevating power. As advertisers are well aware, sex sells, and the perpetuation of the myth that we are still repressed Victorians plays nicely into the machinations of the market. Couple this with another myth, that orgasm is the most authentic experience, and we have a recipe for transforming the pursuit of happiness into the pursuit of the perfect climax. Such a serial and horizontal pursuit closes off the transcending and integrating aspiration of *eros*.

The *pursuit* of happiness has always been problematic. It invites an endless and ultimately unsatisfying search and diverts our attention from the past and the present to the yet-to-be-realized future. Alexis de Tocqueville detected in this phenomenon the source of the peculiar melancholy and restlessness of the American spirit. Nietzsche notes that some may come to find such a pursuit "ridiculous and contemptible." They must undertake a different sort of pursuit or quest amid stifling democratic mores. Spirited people, for example, sometimes find fulfillment in the world of high finance, in unadulterated capitalist competition. In Tom Wolfe's highly successful novel, *The Bonfire of the Vanities*, and in its woeful film version (1990), Wall Street brokers vie to become masters of the universe. The amoralism of that way of life and its attractiveness to the spirited soul is also depicted in the movie *Wall Street* (1987), in which Michael

Douglas delivers his famously blunt speech in praise of raw greed. Although the unrestrained greed of Wall Street would not achieve the highest rank in Nietzsche's hierarchy of values, it comes closer than does socialism. With its morality of selfless altruism, socialism runs counter to the fundamental principle of "growth": "to have and to want to have more."[5] The basic truth of existence is that "a living thing seeks above all to discharge its strength—life itself its will to power; self-preservation is only one of the indirect and most frequent results."[6] When the desire for self-preservation becomes dominant, we are well on our way to nihilism, to emptying human life of all meaning, of any distinction between higher and lower.

The lowly, according to Nietzsche, put pressure on the great to conform to the laws of the majority. Since the slavish soul is timid, fearful, and unable to form an opinion of itself without the assistance of others, it resents independence. Nietzsche depicts the war of the slave against the noble soul thus: "What has been deified? The value instincts in the community. What has been slandered? That which sets apart the highest men from the lowest, the desires that create clefts."[7] The need of most human beings to believe in a moral universe is proof for Nietzsche that lies and self-deception are essential conditions of human life. Once one acknowledges that untruth is a condition of life, one can transcend traditional codes of good and evil. This recognition is closely allied to Nietzsche's famous teaching on the death of God. He does not mean that a supreme being once existed and now has passed out of existence; rather, the human capacity for creating an absolute moral law is also a capacity for the creation of a divinity as the source and guarantor of the law. Nihilism follows the death of God, that is, the growing sense that no religious or moral code is credible. This "pessimism," Nietzsche holds, is but a "preliminary form of nihilism."[8]

Nihilism itself is "ambiguous" between its active and passive forms: the latter is a mark of "decline and recession," while the former is "a sign of increased power."[9] The chaos following the death of God is likely to lead many to despair, to a stagnation of the creative will; in others, it will engender a creative violence greater than that known in any previous age. Thus Nietzsche foresaw that the twentieth century would be a time of unrivaled violence. Unlike many who blithely advocate individual self-creation, as if it could bring about an epoch of harmony and peace, Nietzsche anticipates and readily embraces its destructive consequences. The belief that in order to create one must first destroy leads Nietzsche to celebrate the anti-political virtue of creative boldness—anti-political because it is not subordinate to a common vision of the goods it supposedly defends. The advent of nihilism deprives us of any common vision as it unveils the arbitrariness of all codes of good and evil, and Nietzsche's own project might be seen precisely as the destruction of all previously existing religious and moral codes. The noble soul, which understands its desires as self-justifying, needs no extrinsic justification for such destruction. Nietzsche's great hope is that precisely through the suffering and disorientation of the nihilistic era there will emerge a more profound and higher type of man. He does not believe that the rejection of the slavish distinction of good and evil means that no appraisal of actions or ways of life is possible, but consistently praises the healthy over the sickly soul, ascending over descending patterns of life, and the affirmation over the negation of life.

Echoing Nietzsche's celebration of extremes, Michel Foucault, an advocate of the liberating power of sado–masochistic sexuality, lauds the "limitless presumption of appetite," and counsels the "transcendence of reason in violence." As Roger Shattuck has shown, the great authority in these matters is the Marquis de Sade, who pronounced a "new Gospel" of "crime-connaissance," through creative sexual violence.[10] In Sade's novel *Juliette*, the main character observes that "When one has become accustomed to scorn the laws of nature on one point, one cannot find any pleasure unless one transgresses all of them one after another."[11] Since prohibitions serve only the negative function of enhancing the exhilaration of transgression, the project is subject to the law of diminishing returns. An especially rigorous practice of asceticism is required to revive and intensify the experience of pleasure. The practice of the new Gospel mimics as it inverts the life of Christ. It exercises an asceticism of the body, not for the sake of moderating passions that thwart knowledge and love of others, but for the sake of an ever more refined manipulation of the bodies of others. In lieu of a forgetfulness of self in love of another, "impersonal egoism"—in the words of Bataille—treats the body as a "vile thing." Anyone who stops at theory and fails to embrace this raw, nihilistic truth in practice is a bourgeois coward. Given the bankruptcy of modern politics, of its tidy division of persons into normal and abnormal, the pursuit of evil— at least what society deems evil—is a sign of health.

But there is a tension in Nietzsche between an amoralism that repudiates all objective standards and a distinctively hierarchical kind of thinking that ranks souls on the basis of their vigor, health, power, and creativity. The very distinction between slave and noble morality presupposes a judgment of what is better and worse, higher and lower. Nietzsche simultaneously insists that there is a rank of value and that at the top of that scale resides radical self-creation. By making man the creator, Nietzsche would vindicate the claims of humanity against the Judeo-Christian God. Human creativity will now supplant the transcendent creator of all things *ex nihilo*. Although the blatant hubris of this project renders it comically implausible, the real difficulty is that the exaltation of man as creator seems to relativize all values, leaving nothing in light of which the "revaluation of all values" might occur.

Nietzsche admits that nihilism means "that the highest values devalue themselves," that the "aim is lacking," and that "'why?' finds no answer."[12] Christian morality, still operative in modern politics and, especially, in the naïve faith of Enlightenment science in objective truth, "was the great antidote against . . . nihilism."[13] The disappearance of this antidote means that "Man has lost faith in his own value when no infinitely valuable whole works through him."[14] Nonetheless, Nietzsche forges ahead and invites the crisis as a means of purification, of restoring an "order of rank according to strength."[15] We can see here the reemergence of the model of the virile, heroic warrior, whose distinguishing mark is a creative and courageous boldness, the antithesis of what Nietzsche took to be the feminine, Christian virtues of humility and sympathy. It is a "measure of strength to what extent we can admit to ourselves, without perishing, the merely apparent character" of the world, the "necessity of lies."[16]

It is not surprising that Nietzsche thought of the nihilistic era as tragic, since it would mercilessly lay bare the tremendous tension between, on the one hand, the human aspiration for meaning and purpose and, on the other, the pointlessness of such longings. The virtues that Nietzsche praises—courageous resolve and truthfulness about the non-existence of all objective ideals—are the virtues of those who heroically and tragically confront the emptiness of human life, and there is something noble and edifying in their struggle. It is, however, difficult to sustain the seriousness of the struggle in the face of its meaninglessness. Pointlessness mocks strenuous effort. If no ennobling affirmation emerges from the era of nihilism, the struggle itself comes to seem foolish and laughable. The tragic thus degenerates into a comic satire of all things serious and elevated.

The problem with the project of revaluing all traditional values is not just that it entails the destruction of the weak; it involves a great risk even for the noble soul. However much one might sympathize with Nietzsche's diagnosis of the incredible shrinking modern man, one wonders whether his cure is not worse than the disease. Instead of the affirming way of life that Nietzsche wished to substitute for the negating life of the slave, his apparent exaltation of the will can easily be seen as an essentially negative and empty existence of defying standards and overstepping boundaries. The difficulty, then, with inviting nihilism, the "unwelcome guest," into the heart of civilization is that it deprives us of any grounds for retaining the elevating and ennobling aspect of Nietzsche's thought. The heroic confrontation with nihilism may be inspiring for a time, but its long-term result is likely to be the trivialization of all aspiration, the inability to distinguish between higher and lower. Instead of providing a way to overcome nihilism, Nietzsche's remedy seems only to immerse us more fully in it. By exalting the confrontation of the creative will with nothingness, Nietzsche hoped to revive the grandeur of the tragic hero. But the absence of any goal or standard in light of which we might appraise the hero's life as noble opens the possibility of a comic reversal in our perception of the hero, whose longings now seem silly and farcical.

Another problem with advocating the self-deification of man is his temporality and finitude. The will can only will forward, not backward. All it can do to gain control over what has already happened is to eradicate or alter the influence of the past on the present. This is why destruction is integral to creative activity as Nietzsche understands it. Although it is difficult for us to will the whole of the future, let alone to try to stand outside of time and will the past, present, and the future, this is precisely the strategy that Nietzsche advocates in his doctrine of the eternal recurrence: "Let us think this thought in its most terrible form: existence as it is, without meaning or aim, yet recurring inevitably without any finale of nothingness: the eternal recurrence."[17] In spite of its implausibility, the eternal recurrence captures Nietzsche's sense that the remedy for nihilism involves uprooting from one's soul any vestige of resentment toward life and instead affirming the whole of existence.

Whatever might be the deficiencies of Nietzsche's god-like affirmation of the whole, more modest cyclical journeys can foster growth and development or a new and deeper appreciation of one's point of departure. American film has produced a variety of narratives of the return. There are sentimental versions, as in Dorothy's chant "there's no place like home" in *The Wizard of Oz* (1939). And there are morally serious versions, as in Simba's somber and edifying affirmation of his role in the cycle and hierarchy of nature at the end of *The Lion King* (1994). After the death of his father, Simba's passage from childhood to an adult acceptance of his duty is interrupted. He gets caught in a world of endless adolescence, whose theme song, *Hakuna Matata*, promises no worries, no responsibility, no connection to anything other than immediate gratification. There is an instructive irony here. The chief threat to the moral seriousness *The Lion King* persuasively portrays is the sort of shopping-mall mentality that Disney itself so effectively markets: forgetfulness of the past and the sense that we are no more than our momentary preferences. Consider, by contrast, the pivotal scene in *The Lion King*. Simba's father appears to him, chastises him for neglecting his place, and counsels "You are more than what you have become." His final command, "Remember," resonates throughout the film.

One of the more nuanced variations on the theme of the recurrence is the comedy *Groundhog Day* (1993), which features Bill Murray as a smug, crude, and cynical weatherman sent to cover Groundhog Day festivities in Punxsatawney, Pennsylvania. Murray loathes the town, its people, and their quaint way of life. He cannot wait to leave. But when a snow storm renders the highway out of town impassable, Murray reluctantly returns to town for the night. To his consternation, he awakens the next morning, and for many mornings thereafter, to find himself repeating Groundhog Day. While Murray remembers each previous day, the others in Punxsatawney do not.

He is attracted to the station manager, played by Andie MacDowell, who has accompanied him to Punxsatawney, and devotes each day to some new and increasingly extravagant ruse of seduction. None succeed. Desperate to escape, he resorts to numerous methods of suicide—including some that would take the groundhog out with him—only to awaken yet again in the past. In *Groundhog Day*, the cycle is illustrative of the way vice turns us in on ourselves, stifling freedom and development. Predictably, Murray eventually learns the difference between love and self-gratification and comes to acknowledge the humanity of others. Only after he undergoes a conversion of character does he awaken in and to the future. The irony is that the cycle is the vehicle for the recovery of the self and the overcoming of alienation from others.

Yet without a deep appreciation for and reaffirmation of the past, the cycle becomes what it is in most contemporary drama: a motif for determinism and entrapment. The motif of the futility of the quest pervades our popular culture, and many Americans are plagued by the uneasy sense that large, impersonal forces are at work undermining their search for understanding, love, communion, and meaning. The popularity of horror films that depict evil just beneath the surface of ordinary suburban life belies our confidence in the American experiment. In the *Halloween* and *Friday the 13th* films, for instance, American teenagers—whose youth, good looks, and sexual freedom American culture reveres—are terrorized by a killer who keeps returning.

In such a context, the politics of fear and despair come to the fore. On conservative talk radio, the fear is that our country has been delivered into the hands of socialist despots who have given up on the American dream. Using the overblown and despairing refrain of "America held hostage," Rush Limbaugh inveighs against liberal pessimism. The evening news also plugs into the culture of fear, most obviously in its preoccupation with violent crime, but more insidiously in its endless recitation of the threats to our health and well-being in our food, water, automobiles, schools, and churches. Is it any wonder that conspiracy theories are popular? They are pervasive: from the Left (the films of Oliver Stone and Hillary Clinton's proclamations of right-wing conspiracies) to the Right (fundamentalist cults and separatist militias), and the crudely commercial (*Roswell*) to the subtly artistic (*X-Files*). Ironically, as disturbing as such theories may be, they end up having an oddly consoling effect, relieving the individual of responsibility and subduing his intellect in the face of awesome forces.

Once again, the risk is that fear, terror, and loathing will give way to jaded amusement. So commonplace are the motifs of the horror genre that *Scream* and the inevitable *Scream 2* self-consciously spoof the genre while remaining within it. Thus does the horror at the heart of ordinary American life become a source of comedy. Woody Allen's films are laced with this sort of humor. In the midst of one of his many forays into pop-philosophy, Allen has a desperate character, played by himself, rehearse various philosophical analyses of the meaning of life. He mentions Nietzsche's theory of the eternal recurrence, but flippantly dismisses it: "It wouldn't be worth it. I'd have to sit through the Ice Capades again." Allen's brooding characters never completely break with Nietzsche's philosophical mood and hence never attain a purely comic perspective on nihilism. Precisely this perspective is exploited by sitcoms like *The Simpsons* and, especially, *Seinfeld*, a show about the comical consequences of life in a world void of any ultimate significance or fundamental meaning. *Seinfeld* is, by its own account, a show about nothing.

Nietzsche would, of course, expect such responses from democratic man, who, he contends, is capable of only passive nihilism. But it is hard to see this as an inappropriate response to a philosophy that grounds the future of humanity in the privileged acts of will of the philosopher-artist. Rather than pointing the way toward the overcoming of nihilism, Nietzsche's thought would so fully engulf us in nihilism that the very notion of a way out or a way beyond might come to seem unintelligible and laughable. Nihilism thus simultaneously creates and forecloses possibilities.

AMERICAN CULTURE AND THE UNRAVELING OF THE ENLIGHTENMENT

Before turning to an extended consideration of contemporary popular culture, it may help to have before us a sketch of the development of modern liberalism and America's place in it. This development can be described in terms of three stages in the understanding of the rights and dignity of the individual. Liberalism first expressed its teaching in the social contract, the mutual recognition of rights bestowed on us by virtue of our nature or by God or both. Eventually, liberalism came to view our dignity as grounded in our capacity for self-legislation, beholden to no external authority. Finally, it acknowledged individualism as aesthetic self-creation. How did it move from the first understanding to the third? [18]

The original liberal project grounded the rights of the individual in assertions about nature, or at least about a common human condition, and placed clear limitations upon the exercise of individual rights. Both John Locke's *Two Treatises* and Jefferson's Declaration of Independence appeal to nature and nature's God as the basis of our rights: "We hold these truths to be self-evident: that all men are endowed by their creator with certain inalienable rights." Classical liberalism saw the need to give some sort of account of the source of rights and liberties. Another important feature of the classical view is its insistence that rights have corresponding duties; without this assumption, rights could not be the basis of the liberal social contract.

The Films of Frank Capra

This is the model of American liberalism that dominated the classical period of Hollywood and the early years of television well into the 1960s. The most successful creator of these sorts of American narratives was undoubtedly Frank Capra, who saw his films as vehicles for the communication of an American civil religion. Of *You Can't Take it with You* (1938) he said that it was an opportunity "to dramatize Love Thy Neighbor in living drama. What the world's churches were preaching to apathetic congregations, my universal language of film might say more entertainingly to audiences." In *Mr. Deeds Goes to Town* (1936) and *Mr. Smith Goes to Washington* (1939), Capra juxtaposes the slick, jaded, and conniving denizens of the big city, and especially of the Congress, with the straightforward virtue and simple pleasures of the ordinary, unassuming American citizen. These films put on trial the corruptions and flaws of American democracy, but the accuser is not the cynical loner. He is, rather, the embodiment of the virtues and ideals that America was founded upon and to which it remains tied. Even most of the villains in these films are treated with a comic touch that enables us to perceive their redeeming qualities. The most severe judgment is cast upon the unfeeling capitalism of the usurious Mr. Potter in *It's a Wonderful Life* (1945).

These movies exalt the virtues of old-fashioned American individualism—which really is not individualism at all. Capra often sets an individual, Deeds or Smith, for example, against a group, but the individual himself embodies the ideals that the group is presently falling short of. Capra's films are stories that revive America's founding spirit. In this America, there is no such thing as a completely private life to be disposed of as one wishes. In *It's a Wonderful Life*, George Bailey's attempted suicide is an act of despairing self-absorption. When his guardian angel, Clarence, intervenes to rescue him, George insists that he and everyone else would have been better off had he never existed. Nearly destroyed by his sense of failure, George is the closest anyone comes to nihilism in a Capra film. To instruct George, the angel grants him his wish of non-being, and he learns in painful detail what it means to lack the recognition of neighbors, friends, and family. More positively, he realizes that individualism is a dangerous and destructive illusion, that each life is mysteriously intertwined with many others.

All of these films are comic, even when they include a treatment of serious matters and real evils, and are at least implicitly theological in structure. These films also contain elements of film *noir*. Mr. Smith undergoes tremendous physical and emotional turmoil as he attempts to fight off not only his external, human opponents, the corrupt members of Congress, but also his internal temptation to despair. George Bailey's angel leads him through the city that would have been had he never existed; he must endure the sight of his town turned into a living Hell named Pottersville. If Capra's America is finally an image of paradise, it is always a potential inferno from which art must strive to rescue us.

Just as religions must face the problem of evil in the

world, nations must face its presence in their land. This test has special significance when the nation is America. The most prescient observer of things American, Tocqueville, called democracy a "providential fact" and America, the "image of democracy."[19] As our faith in the American experiment waxes and wanes, so too does faith in the experiment of the modern world. Capra's films are defenses of the essential goodness, and justifications of the ultimate victory, of American democracy. The gravity of evil is never the final word, just as the failure, despair, and isolation of the protagonists are only momentary and apparent. The protagonists embody the American dream and, although they are lowly in the beginning, achieve, just as do the characters in classical comedies, an exalted state. For Capra also, America is a providential fact.

To Kill a Mockingbird

Capra's promulgation of an American civil religion gives legitimacy to the regime and provides a unifying public story. The danger with such stories is that they are too often merely artistic constructs—noble lies—that cover over serious questions. The great modern proponents of civil religion from Hobbes to Rousseau sought to tailor Christianity, the first great non-national religion, to the needs of particular regimes. The American separation of church and state is an ingenious strategy for resolving the problem of an unstable union that was often detrimental to both church and state. But questions about the legitimacy of the regime and its moral unity—precisely the questions civil religions are designed to answer—resurface in times of crisis. The tidy separation of procedural or constitutional issues from so-called issues of value becomes no longer credible. Lincoln was forced to appeal behind the Constitution to the Declaration of Independence, a document which he elevated to the status of American scripture. Echoing Lincoln, Martin Luther King Jr., in his "Letter from a Birmingham Jail," appealed to the Declaration and to the political implications of Christ's proclamation of the kingdom of God. Both Lincoln and King advert to a standard independent of, and prior to, the constitutional principles of the regime.

Both in film and on television, the dramatic justification of the American way of life used to focus on the justice system, especially the courts of law. Tocqueville observed that the court system was so deeply woven into the fabric of American life that children introduce the jury system into their games. That system is an embodiment of the American principle of equality before the law. Of course there have been egregious violations of that ideal in our history. Even when it appears to work well, its success is always tenuous. In according rights to the accused, it risks protecting the guilty rather than the innocent; by insisting on trial by jury, it puts the fate of the accused in the hands of untutored citizens. One film that addresses this inconsistency is *To Kill a Mockingbird* (1962), based on the best-selling and Pulitzer prize-winning novel of the same title by Harper Lee. The film is set in Macon, Georgia, in 1932, where a young black man, Tom Robinson, is falsely accused of raping and beating a white girl. The hero of the story is Atticus Finch, a widowed father of two and the small-town lawyer who defends Tom.

The film is replete with peculiarly American maxims. Atticus explains the term "compromise" to his daughter as an "agreement reached by mutual consent." In so doing, he gives eloquent expression to the principle of the social contract. His summation before the jury invokes Jefferson's great principle of the equality of all citizens. Finch argues that equality has special application to the courts, which are intended to be the "great levelers." But the lessons involve much more than exercises in Enlightenment procedural justice. The title is taken from a story, which Atticus relates to his own children, that his father told him the day he gave him a gun. He would prefer that Atticus shoot only at cans, but since he knew he would eventually get around to shooting birds, his only prohibition was the killing of mockingbirds. It is a sin, Atticus's father tells him, to kill a harmless mockingbird.

Although Atticus is by education and character superior to others in the town, he does not denigrate them, but appreciates their differences in character. To see things from the neighbor's point of view, one has to "crawl around in his skin," he tells his daughter. One has to get to know one's neighbors, who are of different races, religions, and economic status. Not procedures, but a recognition of our common humanity, is the basis of the American regime. The film also teaches lessons in the courageous and restrained facing of violence and willful deception. Atticus and his children are taunted as "nigger lovers"; he is spat on by the drunken father of the alleged victim. Through all this, he remains calm and counsels his children, especially his volatile daughter, Scout, to do the same. In these Hollywood films, courage is not Nietzsche's anti-political virtue, nor is it depicted as sufficient in itself. It serves the maintenance of social order and the protection of the innocent; to succeed it must be accompanied by a host of other virtues.

Mockingbird celebrates American virtues in the ordinary man. Atticus is as concerned about raising his now motherless children as he is about his own career. In fact, his profession is more like a vocation than a career. After he has lost the case, a neighbor comments to his children that some men are "born to do unpleasant jobs." Atticus's virtues, as is generally true of the common man, are most evident in his failures. *Mockingbird*'s affirmation of the American way of life is remarkably restrained, sober, and modest. The pursuit of happiness, the American dream—these themes have no place in this America. Atticus is the embodiment of what Walker Percy calls Southern Stoicism.

Film Noir

Yet even the tragic depiction of America in a film like *Mockingbird* can seem to gloss over American failings—its killing of its own innocent mockingbirds. In this context, the quest for evil can be a healthy response to the naïve and dehumanizing optimism of Enlightenment liberalism. Such a quest is not new to American popular culture. American films of a previous era, especially in film *noir*, took the possibility of nihilism seriously and even flirted with presenting the criminal as an heroic counter to a timid and decadent society. While *noir* productions are markedly different from more recent approaches to nihilism, they do anticipate the contemporary critique of America, its benevolence, its system of justice, its belief in equality and dignity, and its aspiration to happiness.

While there is no consensus on precisely what defines film *noir*, its exemplary instances occur in the post-World

War II period, a period of tremendous success, progress, and growth in America.[20] It was nonetheless a period of unease, uncertainty, and foreboding. While the populist films of that era provide positive visions of American life, film *noir* captures the disconcerting and often suppressed sense that something is deeply awry. It is a dark negation intended to counter the bright affirmation of the public culture of the era. Yet it is never a simple negation. Indeed, film *noir* is both dramatically and artistically complex. Its darkness and shadows, its emphasis on absence over presence, underscore the depth and mystery of the most mundane experiences. Into such a disorienting, threatening, and yet inviting world, *noir* thrusts its would-be hero, who sets out on a quest to solve a particular mystery. But the quest is equally a search for communication, love, and meaning. At a crucial juncture in his journey, the hero is often joined by a woman who, as often as not, ends by deceiving and destroying him. As one critic puts it, *noir* involves a "double quest: to solve the mystery of the villain and of the woman."[21] The modern city, in which the film is usually set, is a kind of labyrinth, which provides a "set of conditions producing a*maze*ment" symbolic of "meaning's multiplicity and elusiveness."[22]

The opening scene of *The Killers* (1946) introduces us to ruthless killers who sit in a diner waiting for the man they plan to murder, Ole Anderson, known as the Swede, played by Burt Lancaster. To employees and customers, they speak with frank brutality: "We're killing him for a friend, just to oblige a friend." After the gunmen leave for the Swede's apartment, a customer rushes to warn him. But he shows no interest in escaping his fate, commenting, "Once I did something wrong." He is murdered, and we are left wondering what he did and why he lost his will to live. An insurance investigator, played by Edmund O'Brien, is our guide to the Swede's life story; the rest of the film is mostly a series of flashbacks prompted by the insurance investigator's interviews with acquaintances of the Swede. The Swede's is a hard-luck story, the tale of a failed boxer who is led by desperation and love to become involved in a heist. A beautiful, but crafty and aloof, woman persuades him that the rest of the gang is plotting to exclude him from the profits and dupes him into stealing the heist money—which she steals from him. The story is not really about the killers, who reappear at the end only to be killed themselves, but about the fragile psyche of the boxer, whom circumstances and unrequited love conspire to destroy.

Film *noir* does not, then, present us with heroes who stand beyond good and evil, but with the seeming impossibility of heroism in a hostile world. It proffers "a disturbing vision . . . that qualifies all hope and suggests a potentially fatal vulnerability."[23] Still, the downfall of the protagonist is not entirely negative. The tragic structure of the would-be hero's quest underscores the gap between his longing for intelligibility, meaning, and love, on the one hand, and his failure to figure things out and achieve salvation, on the other. This longing itself provides the motive force for the drama, for its attempt to "formulate our place in the cultural landscape." Despite its opposition to our simplistic assumptions about shared public meaning, *noir* does not finally treat that aspiration as foolish or silly, but as ennobling. In attempting to speak both of our desire for meaning and of the obstacles to realizing that desire, *noir* effects a "talking cure" and can be seen as an affirmative "genre of life."[24]

The device of the flashback, which we have noted in *The Killers*, is typical of this genre (the *noir* classic *D.O.A.* [1950] consists entirely of an extended flashback). By insisting on the way the past impinges upon the present, the flashback underscores the contingency of the present and future, the way we are held captive by the past. But this is not a fatal determinism, since it prompts a quest through memory to discover the truth about the past, a truth that is never evident but may allow us to endure in the present. According to the conventions of society, the quest and the risks it involves are disproportionate. In *The Killers*, the insurance investigator and his boss joke that his solving of the Swede's case, to which he has devoted inordinate time and energy, will end up saving his company a paltry sum of money. Were he not the best in his field, he likely would have been fired. The levity veils the seriousness of the quest.

By putting our conventions into question, film *noir* opens up the possibility of a more fundamental and more comprehensive inquiry. Its accent on darkness and mystery is an affront to Enlightenment confidence in transparent objectivity and progress. According to the modern conception of progress, we know precisely where we are, where we want to go, and how we are to get there. Film *noir* recovers the premodern conception of life as an always tenuous quest, wherein we are dependent on veiled clues and the uncertain assistance of others. Although fulfillment is never secure, the erotic longing for wholeness and love remain at the very center of the plot. Autonomy is a debilitating illusion, and bold self-assertion, a self-destructive vice. Film *noir* thus engages, without succumbing to, nihilism.

The erotic dimension in film *noir* typically centers on

the female lead. Long before the antinomian *Thelma and Louise* (1991), there was *The File on Thelma Jordan* (1949), starring Barbara Stanwyck, the queen of *noir*. The film opens with a drunk assistant district attorney, played by Wendell Corey, bemoaning his alienation from his family. In walks the seductive Thelma Jordan who gradually draws him into her life; he is unaware that he is a pawn in a plot she has hatched with another man to murder her elderly aunt for her money. Or is he something more than a pawn? The more embroiled she becomes in her own plot and the more the DA, now the prosecutor in her trial for murder, becomes aware of her motives, the more uncertain she seems about where her true allegiance lies. After the DA throws the case and she is acquitted, his hopes for their future together are thwarted by the reappearance of her co-conspirator. But the ending is unhappy for all involved. Thelma is undone not by the law but by the reckless driving of her thug boyfriend, who dies in the crash that leaves her fatally injured. On her deathbed, she issues a double confession—that she committed the murder and that she loves the DA, who has already gone before a judge to accuse himself of subverting justice. The unhappy ending of the film is hardly nihilistic; indeed, the multiple confessions rescue the main characters from the nihilistic web of lies and destruction in which they had entangled themselves.

TOCQUEVILLE AND THE FINAL STAGE OF LIBERALISM

If the first stage of liberalism provides the political and social horizon for the populist Hollywood films of the classical era, the principles of the second stage, an attempt to ground morality and politics in self-legislation, seem to have had little impact on popular culture. According to the chief architect of this position, Immanuel Kant, a democracy is a community of individuals who are simultaneously sovereigns and subjects. No longer is revealed religion, nature, or nature's God an appropriate basis for our self-understanding. Since these are all in some measure extrinsic to the human will, reliance on them is seen to be alienating, an infringement of the dignity of the individual. In Kant's technical language, submission to them puts the individual in a state of "heter-onomy," the exact opposite of autonomy. Kant is remark-ably optimistic about the agreement that is likely to result from everyone's cultivating his autonomy, for he supposes that since each is under his own command, each will ac-knowledge and respect the dignity of the others in their ca-pacity for self-legislation.

It is possible to see a story like *To Kill a Mockingbird* as straddling the first two stages of liberalism. The film makes no reference to God or nature and is replete with lessons about equality and seeing the world from the vantage point of those who are culturally different from us. Yet *Mocking-bird* seems to be of two minds about tradition and cultural particularity. On the one hand, in Kantian fashion, it asks us to prescind from the prejudices of blind tradition and look past the superficial veils of race. On the other hand, the conception of duty that Atticus embodies is infused with the code of honor appropriate to the Southern gentleman. From the Kantian perspective, then, *To Kill a Mockingbird* would be a somewhat impure depiction of the politics of autonomy. That assessment may tell us more about the deficiencies of the model of autonomy than about the dramatic flaws of the film. The problem is that radical autonomy, since it undercuts faith in any objective or communally shared source of morality, easily gives way to nihilism. Once cultural nihilism becomes prevalent, no one has the right or the capacity to determine where the lines ought to be drawn.

In popular culture at least, we jump rather quickly from the first stage of liberalism to the third, in which the notion that universal agreement could arise from personal autonomy is seen to be preposterous. Nietzsche believes the third stage of liberalism a secularized and impoverished version of Christian morality, a tenuous middle ground between the Christian worldview and the unleashing of a more radical conception of freedom. As he puts it, the "terms autonomous and moral are mutually exclusive."[25] In its break with external authority, the second stage of liberalism paves the way for a doctrine of freedom as unfettered self-expression, as the creation of value. The logical conclusion of this doctrine is on display in the pro-drug comedy *Trainspotting* (1996), in which the main character describes the decision of his friends to use heroin as a fully-informed, democratic choice.

In spite of the surprising impact of Nietzsche's anti-political principles on American thought and culture, Nietzsche himself remains something of an outsider, little understood in the culture he has helped shape. It is unlikely, for instance, that he will ever be given the attention that C-SPAN recently devoted to Alexis de Tocqueville and his *Democracy in America*. Yet we find in his work a startling anticipation of Nietzsche's prophesies about the epoch of political equality, especially about how certain forms of liberalism naturally generate nihilism. According to Tocqueville, there are two dominant passions in democracy: the love of liberty and the love of equality, the more powerful of which is the latter. When allied to the longing for physical well-being, the passion for equality leads to a remarkable sameness of condition and to uniformity of opinion even as it dissipates the soul by immersing it in the pursuit of consumer goods and petty pleasures.

In political discourse, liberalism has come to be associated with big government, and this might seem antithetical to the account of liberalism as always potentially radically individualist. Liberalism was indeed founded on the principle of limited government, which leaves local communities and intermediate level institutions free to develop in common their own ways of living together. Tocqueville thought that Americans could resist the twin dangers of centralization and individualism only so long as they participated in democratic life, only so long as they were what *The Federalist* calls an "active and engaged citizenry." But the passion for equality and well-being can be at variance with the spirit of liberty. It leads citizens to welcome the intrusion of government into every aspect of daily life to rectify wrongs and to equalize the unequal. The weakening of the ties between the individual and local, mediating institutions creates a political and existential vacuum.

If citizens abdicate their responsibility for self-government, they are all-too-willing to permit government to perform a vast array of functions on their behalf. Thus do centralization and individualism reinforce one another. The battle between big-government Democrats and libertarian Republicans, for example, fosters the diminution of man and overlooks important social phenomena. Cornell West argues, for instance, that both sides fail to come to terms with, or even adequately to acknowledge, the basic threat to the black community in America, the "nihilistic threat." Neither the "liberal structuralist" focus on government programs nor the "conservative behaviorist" call for individual responsibility addresses the "loss of hope and the absence of meaning."[26] As experienced in the black community, nihilism is not so much a philosophical doctrine as a "lived experience of coping with a life of horrifying meaninglessness, hopelessness, and (most important) lovelessness."

There is, then, a hidden alliance between centralized government and individualism. They are mirror images of one another; each tends to give birth to its opposite. How are we to understand the relationship? According to Tocqueville, "When the inhabitant of a democratic country compares himself individually with all those about him, he feels with pride that he is the equal of any one of them; but when he comes to survey the totality of his fellows and to place himself in contrast with so huge a body, he is instantly overwhelmed by the sense of his own insignificance and weakness. The same equality that renders him independent of each of his fellow citizens, taken severally, exposes him alone and unprotected to the influence of the greater number."[27] The impotence of the individual before the whole of society makes possible a hitherto unknown form of tyranny, a "new physiognomy of servitude." The great danger is not, as it was in previous eras, the despotism of a single man or even of a class. We witness

> an innumerable multitude of men, all equal and alike, incessantly endeavoring to procure the petty and paltry pleasures with which they glut their lives. Each of them, living apart, is a stranger to the fate of all the rest; his children and his private friends constitute to

him the whole of mankind. . . . Above this race of men stands an immense and tutelary power, which takes upon itself alone to secure their gratification and to watch over their fate. That power is absolute, minute, regular, provident, and mild. It would be like the authority of a parent, if . . . its object were to prepare men for manhood; but it seeks, on the contrary, to keep them in perpetual childhood. . . . For their happiness such a government willingly labors. . . . what remains, but to spare them all the care of thinking and all the trouble of living?[28]

What sort of citizens does such a regime produce? Tocqueville does not give them a name, but it would be hard to distinguish them from Nietzsche's last men. According to Tocqueville, these enervated souls suffer from the shrinking of each person's world to a very small circle. Some social conservatives might be surprised to learn that what they call family values and see as an alternative to liberal individualism is nearly indistinguishable from what Tocqueville calls individualism: "a mature and calm feeling, which disposes each member of the community to sever himself from the mass of his fellows and to draw apart with his family and his friends, so that after he has thus formed a little circle of his own, he willingly leaves society at large to itself."[29]

Tocqueville, the most prescient analyst of American democracy, anticipates many of Nietzsche's insights about the subtle link between democratic liberalism and nihilism, even if he rejects Nietzsche's anti-political corrective. Instead, he advocates ways to temper our passion for equality of condition and physical well-being. More important than institutional structures and constitutional principles are the customs and mores of democratic nations. He thought it was crucial that popular mores invigorate individuals with a sense of the grandeur of life in a democracy and that it present examples of the virtues and sacrifices necessary to keep alive the spirit of liberty. Without being explicitly religious, popular culture should contain a kind of civil religion that teaches us to cherish, love, and care for our common life. It should also draw us out of our concentration on the present and our immersion in the limited circle of family and friends to take a long-term view of our lives and to participate in the political life of the nation.

Both Nietzsche and Tocqueville see the problem as more than a matter of altering the structure of political regimes. The underlying difficulty is one of mores or habits, arising from a shift in the understanding of the place of humanity in the universe. We can see this transformation best in the modern idea of scientific and technological progress. For all its undisputed contributions to our understanding of the universe, science often undermines the dignity of the individual so prized by modern political theory. Think of the way Darwin's theory of evolution demotes human beings from their traditional rank in the universe, or of the way Freud's theories reduce conscious, rational life to the subconscious and irrational, or of the way contemporary biology explains all our apparently free decisions in terms of physical-chemical processes. If there is nothing especially distinctive or noble about human beings, then on what grounds do we celebrate their intrinsic dignity?

Further complicating matters is the stance of Enlightenment science toward the world. One of its fundamental goals was succinctly articulated by the seventeenth-century French philosopher and scientist René Descartes. The end of science, he writes, is to "render us masters and possessors of nature." This ambitious, one might say hubristic, project has given rise to numerous crises, not the least of which is the insoluble question of the place of humanity in nature. To master and control nature would seem to entail our standing above or outside it, even against it. Where do we fit in? Do we have any natural place within the world? And what, if any, are the limitations to our project of mastery? The result of modern science's view of nature as raw material, to be disposed of at our discretion, is the alienation of humanity from the world.

Here we confront the "dread chasm that has rent the soul of Western man ever since . . . Descartes ripped body lose from mind and turned the very soul into a ghost that haunts its own house."[30] Consider, for example, the Human Genome Project which has been described as the "grail of human genetics . . . the ultimate answer to the commandment, 'Know thyself.'"[31] In this case, knowledge is equivalent to power. By knowing our origins, we can determine our future. The irony, lost on the scientists, is that in the process "we" will have vanished. If the self is but a genetic code and if the code can be altered at our discretion, then the self is something even less substantial than Descartes's ghostly ego. In his comical lack of self-reflection, the scientist fails to ask the questions: Who or what is knowing the code, and who or what is deciding how it should be emended? Wouldn't it be an embarrassingly hollow answer, demeaning to the dignity of the scientist, to say that a code is being known by a code? Scientific indifference to these issues confirms Nietzsche's suspicion that Enlightenment science will bring us face to face with our own nothingness. The admonition of Montaigne and Pascal that whoever strives to be an angel ends up a beast now seems naïve. At least a beast is something.

In jettisoning authority—indeed, the past itself—Enlightenment progress is supposed to liberate the individual. But progress puts the individual at the service of large, impersonal, historical forces. Tocqueville worried that the modern emphasis on historical progress would engender in individuals a sense of helplessness and impotence born of the suspicion that the actions and thoughts of an individual are as nothing in comparison with the force of history.

PERPETUAL ADOLESCENCE

Numerous hidden and powerful forces, then, conspire to render human life small and insignificant. A state of perpetual childhood, Tocqueville fears, may result not only from encroaching centralized power, but also from the absence of any clear notion of what it means to be a mature human being. Their claims to foster personal growth notwithstanding, contemporary self-help guides exacerbate the problem. Given the absence of any criteria in light of which one might distinguish between progress and regress, growth and decay, their language is bankrupt. Indeed, their effect is often to bring about a kind of paralysis of the will, an inability to make any long-term commitments. The project of creating a self *ex nihilo* leads to a restless uncertainty about the future and the frenetic and violent process of making and unmaking decisions.

Here, the deconstructed self of postmodern philosophy converges with the evanescent self of the stars of prime-time television: for example, Ally McBeal and the main characters of the sitcom *Seinfeld*. The result is a kind of perpetual adolescence, a natural consequence of the disappearance of any clear model of adult life, of what it might mean to grow or develop from a child into an adult. Too often the passage means simply that without external intervention we may now do as we please. But, once we reach a certain age, society expects us to conform to some of the external trappings of adult life. The curse is that the fragility of the self precludes bold rebellion and fosters timid conformity. From *Married . . . with Children* to *Dawson's Creek,* adults on television are but unsuccessful adolescents whose time has come and gone.

The Hollywood of classic films had clear notions of the differences between childhood and adulthood and of the appropriate paths from the former to the latter. Like the sitcoms of its era, *To Kill a Mockingbird* often succeeds best at depicting the world of children. The entire story is told from the perspective of Scout, who is just six years old at the time of the events. The epigraph to the book is from Charles Lamb: "Lawyers, I suppose, were children once." This is a world that is generally safe for children, not because there are no threats to their well-being and not because every child comes from a well-adjusted home with a happily married mother and father: the Finch children are motherless. It is safe because there is a community ordered to the raising of children that is generally agreed on the essential virtues that need to be inculcated in them. This sense of communal responsibility for children also realizes itself in certain predictable vices—snooping, gossip, and unwelcome and imprudent intrusions—that are better articulated in the book than in the movie.

The ability to invoke the life of children has almost completely vanished from Hollywood. Most children in contemporary movies sound like adults trying to sound like children. While Disney supplies films for the very young, there is almost nothing for children between that age and adolescence. In this, Hollywood reflects the worst segments of our society, in which childhood has completely vanished and carried adulthood along with it. What replaces both of these is a state of arrested adolescent development—our contemporary compromise between the two dominant conceptions of childhood. The Enlightenment viewed childhood as an obstacle to be overcome at all costs. Since youth is the time of our greatest dependence on tradition and authority, when others largely do our thinking for us, it is the antithesis of the Enlightenment ideal of autonomy. A chief exponent of this line of thought is Descartes: "I thought that we were all children before being men, at which time we were necessarily under the control of our appetites and our teachers, and that neither of these influences is wholly consistent, and neither of them, perhaps, always tend to the better. It is therefore impossible that our judgments should be as pure and firm as they would have been had we the use of our reason from the time of our birth and if we had never been under any other control."[32]

Descartes's corrective is to repudiate every opinion he has inherited from others, to destroy the entire edifice of his beliefs and rebuild knowledge upon a more firm foundation. The passage is an early statement of the goals of liberal Enlightenment and scientific progress. One must extirpate the influence of tradition, convention, and authority from one's reasoning, act autonomously, dare to use one's reason by and for oneself.

Reacting against the alienating, degrading, and dispiriting consequences of the Enlightenment, nineteenth-century Romanticism presented an alternative ideal. It exalted instinct and imagination over reason, spontaneity and poetry over calculation and science. The Romantic celebration of the natural innocence of the pre-civilized child recurs as a model of goodness in contemporary American popular culture. The new problem of evil is essentially a problem of goodness, of the absence of models of virtue and excellence. In movies like *Forrest Gump* (1994) and *Rain Man* (1989), we discover Hollywood's present-day penchant for equating goodness with insuperable innocence and perpetual childhood. A mental disability actually frees one from the corruptions of civilized adult life.

The ideal of the noble savage or innocent child is but one side of Romanticism, a historically complex phenomenon. The Romantic model of innocent goodness is not the dominant contemporary alternative to Enlightenment rationality. Instead, autonomy resurfaces in the form of aesthetic self-creation and in the fascination with the awe-inspiring manifestations of a demonic power that resides beyond good and evil. The model of aesthetic self-creation is itself an offshoot of a rival, Romantic conception of nature, for the assumption of nature as naïvely innocent and wholesome seems quickly to have generated the opposite view that nature is demonic. In much of nineteenth-century Romantic poetry, one can find juxtaposed to the representation of nature as undefiled, innocent, and pacific, an image of nature as wild, excessive, and frantic, as a superabundant source of life and creativity, a source that eludes the categories of reason and morality. The duality of nature is a commonplace, for instance, of Blake's poetry; the amoral image of nature saturates Coleridge's "Kubla Kahn." Contemporary film also alternates between celebrating inviolable innocence and seeing youth as predatory villains—the tragedy of *Dead Poets Society* and *Titanic*, on the one hand, and the *Child's Play* and *Halloween* films, on the other. Life has regrettably begun to imitate art in the frightening explosion of child murderers and schoolyard assassins, many of whom, recall, purport to have been influenced by Nietzsche and contemporary film. Thus does one strain of Romanticism, like certain strains of Enlightenment liberalism, prepare a path to nihilism.

THE REVENGE OF THE DARK GOD

Nietzsche traces the origin of nihilism to the death of the Judeo-Christian God, to the vanishing of the supernatural from human life. In fact, Nietzsche believes the seeds of nihilism are latent in the Judeo-Christian story. By opposing this world to the next, passion and instinct to divine law, and denigrating the former in favor of the latter, the Judeo-Christian religion empties this life of significance. It is essentially an anti-vital principle.

But Nietzsche is too hasty here. It is possible to trace the religious roots of nihilism, not to the original Judeo-Christian view of God, but to a distortion of it in the late medieval and early modern period. A certain conception of divinity, which arose with voluntarism and nominalism in the late medieval era, accentuates God's absolute freedom and power and thus sees him as all-powerful, arbitrary, and capricious. There is no intrinsic, intelligible link between the world and God, between human and divine morality. Nature either becomes mute or speaks in convoluted and contradictory ways; it is no longer a book in which, with the help of Scripture, we might read the signs of divine art.

It does not take much imagination to detect similarities between an omnipotent, arbitrary deity and the contemporary anti-hero who displays his creative power in capricious acts of destruction. This is the dark God whose possible influence Descartes sought to eliminate. Assaulted by doubts, Descartes wanted to find a sure and useful foundation for all knowledge, especially for scientific knowledge. As a means of gaining absolute and unshakable certitude, he proposed to subject all his beliefs to the most stringent standards of proof. Any belief that allows for a degree of doubt must be set aside. For example, sense-experience is at times deceptive, so we must discount it entirely. For similar reasons, Descartes questions the existence of all external objects, other persons, even his own body. Having dismissed all this, he goes on to consider whether he might be deceived even about apparently certain truths like those of mathematics. For the sake of argument, he postulates the existence of "not a God, who is the supreme source of truth, but a certain evil spirit, not less clever and deceitful than powerful, [who] has bent all his efforts to deceive me." Descartes famously thought that he might be able to compete with such a deity or at least that he could carve out a realm of knowledge immune to the tricks of such a being: "I . . . shall prepare my mind so well for all the ruses of this great deceiver that, however powerful and artful he may be, he will never be able to mislead me in anything." This leads to his notorious argument that, even if he is being deceived, at least he is sure of this much—that "it is [he who] is being deceived." Since his being deceived presupposes his thinking and his existence, he is immune to deception about one truth: "I think, therefore I am."[33]

Descartes's victory is Pyrrhic; he wins only at the cost of sacrificing the external world, his body, and other persons. The hollow self that remains anticipates the flimsy sense of self possessed by the last men. According to Nietzsche and many others, Descartes failed to achieve the goal of rational enlightenment: he never conquered the dark god. Our inheritance is dualism and skepticism. Cut adrift from the bodily, natural world, we lose our bearings, anxiously suspect that nothing is substantial, and latch on to the body as providing an indubitable experience of the real. The more forceful and more intense is our encounter with the body, the less are we able to doubt the world or ourselves.

The preoccupation with the malignant evil genius is present not only in Descartes, the founder of modern philosophy, but also in Hobbes, the founder of modern political science. His famous state of nature is an amoral universe in which every individual pursues a "restless desire for power after power." This is the war of all against all. The way out of this situation, which is suffused with the fear of violent death, is through a social compact wherein each cedes his natural rights in order to gain peace. The compact vests the right to make and enforce law in a Leviathan, or absolute ruler. Although his legitimacy is grounded in the original act of the consent of the ruled, the Leviathan's unencumbered freedom to determine law and punishment is similar to God's right to rule by his "irresistible power."[34] We owe him obedience not as a "gracious creator" but as an omnipotent ruler.

Descartes thought he could forestall the deceptions of the dark god, while Hobbes sought to ground a rational science of politics on such a conception of divinity. Both projects saddle us with a dilemma. Since this god is not necessarily good or just, it is not a god that one could reasonably worship. It is not clear what would satisfy him: perhaps worship, perhaps indifference, perhaps hostility. One possible response is to combat this deity by engaging in a battle of wills. We may not be made in the image of a benevolent, provident God, but we can still cultivate the detachment and malevolent humor of the dark god.

Though the ideal of autonomous self-creation, an *imitatio diaboli,* does not dominate the daily lives of average Americans as it does the culture of Hollywood, it does play an increasingly prominent role in our public discourse, especially in our intractable debates over rights and liberties. Once radical autonomy takes hold it is hard to resist its nihilistic implications. As we noted above, the art of American film has often taken the possibility of nihilism quite seriously; our inability to overcome it completely instructs us about the insuperable limitations of American life. Although the search for explanation and meaning is unfulfilled or ends tragically, it remains an ennobling imperative. The advent of democratic nihilism threatens to deprive us of any shared vision—or even the aspiration for a vision—the absence of which creates a social, political, and artistic vacuum.

But society, even more than nature, abhors a vacuum. Many worry that our contemporary popular culture is confused, chaotic, and destructive, although they may not call our age nihilistic. It would be wrong, however, to think that the influence of nihilism leads to chaos and anarchy. Nihilism is a kind of limit, which we can approach asymptotically but never reach, for there is no utterly shapeless life. The paradox of nihilism is that it generates more determinate and mechanistic social forms. Thus the complexity, depth, and flexibility appropriate to human life are lost. What we now lack are complex and nuanced depictions of goodness or of the struggle between good and evil in a weak and flawed but nonetheless admirable, or at least pitiable, soul.

A culture on the cusp of nihilism, by turns apprehensive, frightened, and exhilarated at the prospect of being beyond good and evil—such a culture might be said to illustrate the new problem of evil. The old problem of evil was both a philosophical difficulty and an existential quandary. The question could be phrased variously: Why do bad things happen to good people?. Or conversely, Why to good things happen to bad people? Or in more precise philosophical language, How is the presence of evil compatible with the goodness of existence, and especially with presence of a good, all-powerful, and all-knowing God? The existence of evil used to be a problem precisely because we were reasonably clear about the difference between evil and goodness. Even if skeptics or atheists did not assume the existence of God, they did assume that everyone could tell the difference between good and evil; otherwise, their objection would be either without merit or unnecessary. The new problem is not that the meaning of evil is elusive, but that it is increasingly difficult for us to distinguish between evil and goodness.

So commonplace is the dramatic depiction of evil, especially in its demonic form, that it has made its way to prime time, with a flood of movies-of-the-week devoted to serial killers and with television series like *Millennium*. In these shows, the quest for evil and its eradication is pushed to ultimate questions and issues. While this opens up new possibilities of explanation, it also is attended by certain problems. There is a lack of scale or measure in the depiction of evil; put in such large terms, the questions are insoluble and the quest itself risks becoming pointless. Often the existence of Satan is much more evident than that of God. But without a God to rebel against, even Satan's motives become a bit murky.

DEAD ENDS, WAYS OUT, AND PATHS THROUGH

In many recent films, the evildoer displays his courage, independence, and power by setting himself in opposition to a homogenized, timid, and conformist society. He performs deeds intended to offend, shock, and repulse ordinary law-abiding citizens. Yet these same deeds also attract and inspire ordinary folk, since they too have begun to see through the ideals of the Enlightenment. In contemporary films, the Enlightenment disciplines of law enforcement and behaviorist psychology are subject to relentless and unqualified critique. In response to the reduction of evil to psychosomatic illness, contemporary films set out on a quest for evil, for deeds so heinous that all efforts at scientific explanation fall comically short. Although there are many sources of this new view of evil, *The Exorcist* (1973) merits special attention. This film, which made horror respectable, contains the seeds of all the themes just mentioned. More than any popular film in recent history, *The Exorcist* leads us patiently to a confrontation with the Devil. It takes the quest seriously and asserts the primacy of religious and mythical accounts of evil over that of Enlightenment science. All this makes the film a serious and potentially edifying exploration of evil. But, even as it strives to vindicate the ultimate power of goodness, it unleashes the complex and powerful forces associated with the aesthetics of evil. These forces are brought to fruition not so much in films of the horror genre itself as in more mainstream and critically acclaimed movies like *Cape Fear* and *Silence of the Lambs* (both 1991). These stories exalt the artistic boldness of their evil supermen, who put into question the timid mores of conventional society and resist its standard mechanisms for understanding, punishing, and rehabilitating criminals. In such a context, evil begins to appear attractive, courageous, and liberating.

Although these films contain scenes that echo the *noir* genre, they depart from it in crucial ways. They bring evil out into the light of day, divest it of its mystery, and thus undermine the motives for the quest. The erotic element is either nonexistent or is allied to acts of perversity and violence. Thus the longing for communication, love, and meaning is not so much thwarted as displaced and dismissed. In the absence of such longing, a tragic approach to evil or the human condition cannot be sustained.

After *Cape Fear* and *Silence*, where do we go? Most productions simply continue in the same direction and try to distinguish themselves by giving the audience more of the same, increasing the deployment of grotesque and offensive language, deeds, and situations. But this strategy is subject to the law of diminishing returns. As the detachment and irony of the audience increase, it becomes desensitized to evil, which ceases to terrify and becomes funny. To put it more precisely, we should say that the aesthetics of evil now inspire both fear and laughter. We have entered the genre of what one critic calls the "comic beat of never-ending terror."[35] There are hints of this already in *Cape Fear* and *Si-*

lence, even in *The Exorcist*. Scorsese himself said of his version of *Cape Fear*, "It's a picture about a man who wants revenge. And it's a lot of fun."

The consequence is that evil, which starts out as the new path to freedom, as an attractive and exciting way to overcome conventional society, manifests its own essential emptiness and banality. With uncharacteristic wit, Charles Manson captured this when he responded to Diane Sawyer's question whether he was crazy: "Sure I'm crazy. Being crazy used to mean something. Nowadays everybody's crazy." If rebellion fails to produce some alternative standard, it becomes pointless and frivolous. All that is left is the aesthetics of evil, whose techniques are increasingly explicit and incredible. As the audience becomes conscious of the artifice, it gains distance from the effects of evil, which is transformed into pure entertainment. This is the route taken in recent films like *Natural Born Killers* (1994), *Trainspotting* (1996), and *Pulp Fiction* (1994). These are sometimes labeled dark comedies, but for all the violent destructiveness of these films, they do not treat evil as a dark, mysterious force at all, but rather as conventional, almost ordinary.[36] They represent a stage in the movement toward a purely comic take on evil.

Courageous resolve, so prominent in the earlier films, is replaced by the erotics of evil, the sheer delight in transgression. But the return of *eros* does not necessarily bring with it a revitalized sense of the search for love, meaning, and communication. If we follow the aesthetics of self-creation through to its logical term, the life of evil comes to resemble the trivial world of conventional society. In *Pulp Fiction*, gangster and drug life are indistinguishable from ordinary society. The final stage, then, in the artistic response to the advent of cultural nihilism is to see the very distinction between conventionalism and radicalism as itself absurd. Both traditional morality and the courageous anti-hero are incredible. This route adopts, defends, and celebrates the life of the last man against all alternatives. This, I think, is the path taken by the most successful television show of the 1990s, *Seinfeld*, a show about "absolutely nothing." It is instructive that both Jerry Seinfeld and Quentin Tarantino, author of the original script for *Killers* and director of *Pulp Fiction*, see reflections of their own work in that of the other. *Seinfeld*'s comic nihilism is a remarkably creative take on the comical consequences of life in a world lacking any ultimate purpose or basic meaning. It also illustrates the way nihilism exercises a subtle but extensive influence in our popular culture.

It might seem, then, that the great quest for evil has reached an impasse, that the confrontation with evil is unable to generate an ennobling new world. The secret is out: Evil is nothing. Our response? Adolescent giggling. Ironic, detached comedy provides a way out of the pain and despair of our condition, but this is pure escapism. If this were the whole story, we would indeed have reached a dead end. Contemporary art is more resourceful than this pessimistic judgment allows, however. One thing is clear: there is no easy way back to Enlightenment ideals. As we shall see, when contemporary art seeks to find a way through the misery and seeming chaos of contemporary life, it does so by reviving the classical, premodern conception of life as a quest in both tragic (*Seven*) and comedic (*Pulp Fiction*) versions.

2

The Quest for Evil

THE AESTHETIZATION OF EVIL is now a given in Hollywood, where allegiance has shifted from victims and societal order to sympathy with the devil. Moral ambiguity and black comedy are not new to the world of American film. Both trends can be found in film *noir* and in popular Hitchcock movies. What is new is the pervasiveness of this approach to evil and the grotesque brutality that accompanies it. Also unrivaled is the critique of conventional society and the confidence with which demonic characters are celebrated for their courageous and creative transcendence of the categories of good and evil. Since the release of *The Exorcist* (1973) we have been inundated by horror films. Many of these explore in detail the themes of the aesthetics of evil, the villain-hero who exists beyond good and evil, and the impotence of the American systems of justice and psychiatric medicine. *The Exorcist, Cape Fear*, and *Silence of the Lambs* contain all these themes, though they do not fit neatly into a single genre. With the possible excep-

54

tion of *Cape Fear*, all achieved a certain measure of critical acclaim; all have gained a wider audience than that of the typical horror film. Their influence is far-reaching; scenes from these films have become ingrained in our cultural memory. Given their heterogeneity, what makes these movies appropriate vehicles for exploring the new problem of evil in popular culture?

In spite of their differences, these films exhibit underlying similarites in themes and strategies. The demonic villain takes center stage, and his personality transfixes the audience. By means of didactic speeches and grotesquely offensive acts, all these incarnations of evil mock fundamental features of contemporary American life: the cowardly mores of conventional society, the arbitrary system of American justice, and the intellectual poverty of our standard mechanisms, especially that of behaviorist psychology, for understanding evil. In each case, the evildoer is invulnerable to our morality, our punitive threats, and our attempts at explanation. American society is feeble, shallow, and complicit in the very evil that it supposedly wants to eradicate.

Cultural critics bemoan these attacks on civility and traditional morality, and they may well be right about the corrosive effect of these attacks on American culture. But these critics too often misconstrue the target of these films, which they assume to be the segment of American society committed to so-called traditional values. Wittingly or unwittingly, the real target of these movies is Enlightenment politics and science. The utopian, rationalist vision of the Enlightenment, luring us with the promise of eliminating both physical and moral evil, is no longer credible. Contemporary horror films mercilessly unveil the bankruptcy of contemporary sociology, law, and psychology—all Enlightenment disciplines.

In Walker Percy's novel *Lancelot*, the protagnoist rejects an America where evil is explained away, where the vast majority believe in the existence of God, but almost none can say what difference that belief makes. A modern Lancelot, he sets out in search of the Unholy Grail: evil itself. He justifies his quest thus: "Have you ever considered that one might undertake a search not for God but for evil? You people have been on the wrong track all these years with all that talk about God and signs of his existence, the order and beauty of the universe—that's all washed up. . . . The more we know about the beauty and order of the universe, the less God has to do with it. . . . But what if you could show me a *sin*? a purely evil deed, an intolerable deed for which there is no explanation? Now there's a mystery."[1] If good and evil are classified merely in terms of the normal and the abnormal or the exceptional, then real evil no longer exists. Everyone is "either wonderful or sick." The search for palpable evil, in which profoundly conservative authors like Dostoevsky, T. S. Eliot, and Walker Percy have engaged, may be the only meaningful quest left to us. Of course, it is always possible that the search may fail, the quest lead nowhere, and that confronting malignant forces may dissipate rather than deepen our sense of the mystery of evil. As I shall argue in the next chapter, that failure may be instructively turned to profit, since the nothingness of evil returns us to classical insights about the nature of both evil and goodness. But before addressing the topic of the emptiness of evil, we need to see how the aesthetics of evil plays itself out.

THE QUEST BEGINS: *The Exorcist*

The Exorcist (1973), William Friedkin's production of William Peter Blatty's best-selling novel, was an unprecedented film in a number of ways. Conflating two traditional genres—the fantastic horror film and the realistic murder mystery—it was one of the first horror films to achieve mainstream popularity. Widespread reports of patrons showering theater bathrooms with vomit and later seeking therapy testify to its impact on audiences. Filled with grotesque images and terrifying sounds, the film was ahead of its time. Its sensationalism transported the audience out of the world of everyday vices and into the dramatic world of supernatural evil. Although in the end the exorcism succeeds and the girl is freed from the clutches of evil, the movie persistently flirts with glamorizing evil, a tendency that was to be fully embraced in subsequent films. The analysis of evil within an explicitly religious context gives *The Exorcist* a distinct advantage over its successors. The quest is clear: locate the evil; name, define, constrain, and ultimately purge it. The framework for the quest is the medieval, Catholic sacramental system with its complex rituals, signs, and symbols. After the film's release, debate raged about the clarity, consistency, and dramatic efficacy of its religious teaching. Yet despite its flaws, the film wants desperately to glimpse the hand of God at work in the human confrontation with evil.

The film now seems almost tame by comparison with the excesses one has come to expect in an average horror film. Regan's projectile vomiting and other displays of satanic power do not begin until nearly halfway through the film. Such a postponement is now rare. The movie also takes the introduction and development of its characters seriously. We are made aware of the way various contingent circumstances bring a group of individuals together for an encounter with evil that will be the definitive moment in their lives. The opening segment of the film thus implicitly asks the key questions: who is orchestrating these events, and is the power malignant or benign?

The opening third of the movie also builds a sense of impending disaster. We meet the family of Regan MacNeil, the only child of divorced parents. Her mother, Chris, a famous Hollywood actress, is on location in Georgetown. An early scene, on Regan's birthday, has her mother failing to contact Regan's father, who is away in Europe with another woman. As her anger and frustration swell, Chris curses Regan's father in words overheard by Regan. Regan expresses her anxiety over her absent father indirectly by inquiring about her mother's relationship with the director of her movie, Burke Dennings. Chris feebly tries to assuage Regan's worries, but her mood runs counter to her assurances. The setting for the exchange is Regan's invitation to her mother to join her in playing with her new imaginary friend, Captain Howdy, on the ouija board. Lacking human affection and communication, Regan conjures up an apparently make-believe friend.

Through the strategy of subtle but cumulative suggestion, we are led slowly into a confrontation with evil. Increasingly strange sounds, emanating from behind Regan's closed bedroom door, repeatedly call her mother (and us) up a staircase, down a hallway, and into her room. With each trip, we mark the growing alienation of Regan from the public world and are gradually enveloped by an insidious and inexplicable force. The evil is evident at a cast party held at the MacNeil house early in the movie. Without provocation or evidence, a drunken Dennings belligerently accuses MacNeil's German servant of being a nazi. (Dennings is later pressed into service to watch over Regan and is found dead at the bottom of those famous steps with his head twisted around.)

The inexplicability of evil is indirectly portrayed in the only scene that shows us MacNeil at work on her movie. As Dennings prepares to shoot a scene about a student rebellion on the campus of Georgetown University, a producer, played by Blatty, asks, "Is the scene really essential, Burke? Would you just consider it, whether or not we could do without it?" To this question, MacNeil adds one of her own concerning the motives of the student protesters: "Well, why are they tearing the building down?" Dennings answers only Chris's question: "Shall we summon the writer? He's in Paris, I believe." To which Chris responds, "Hiding?" This film within the film subordinates the question about the motives for rebellion and destruction to the question of who is in charge of the script and what his intentions are. This turns our attention to the author of *The Exorcist* and the author of the story of human life, namely, God. The question whether God speaks in *The Exorcist* is never unequivocally answered.

In the first part of the film, Blatty and Friedkin apply T. S. Eliot's principle that the "religious mind works by exclusion," carefully setting up and then puncturing the dominant, secular account of evil. It is the account proffered by Enlightenment science, which reduces evil either to antecedent, external influences, such as childhood trauma, or to underlying somatic illness. The method meets the audience on its own terms. Because Regan's family has no religious beliefs, they begin where most Americans begin, by seeking out the psychosomatic roots of the girl's growing disorder. The doctors methodically attempt, first, to "exhaust the somatic possibilities" and then to trace her illness to a "lesion in the temporal lobe." When neither diagnosis offers any hope of a cure, the doctors concede that exorcism has an "outside chance of a cure" as a kind of "shock treatment." The disorder, one doctor explains in dispassionate and clinical terms, is rooted in conflict and guilt. Since the patient suffers from a "delusion of invasion," the exorcism may work "purely through the force of suggestion."

Abandoning medical science, Chris MacNeil introduces herself to Father Karras, a Jesuit psychiatrist from Georgetown University, and then abruptly inquires how one would go about getting an exorcism. An incredulous Karras responds that the first thing Chris would have to do is to travel in "a time machine back to the sixteenth century." We simply do not use exorcism now that we know about various psychological disorders—"all the things they taught me at Harvard." The scene sets up the battle between medieval Catholicism and modern, Enlightenment science, with its eschewal of religion as superstition. Although the movie takes seriously the claims of modern science to explain certain kinds of disorder, it reverses the modern, hierarchical relationship of science and religion. At one point, the film alternates between scenes of Father Karras saying Mass and the doctors' performing a rather gruesome series of tests on Regan. The Mass is depicted at the moment of consecration, when the bread and wine become the body and blood of Christ. It commemorates Christ's personal, sacrificial offering of his body for sinful mankind. At the same moment, in the hospital, Regan, observed from afar by a team of doctors, is injected with dye and inserted into a variety of monitoring devices. The dispassionate and impersonal manner in which Regan's body is subjected to the instruments of medical science is excruciating to watch.

More than any other character, Karras mediates between the audience and the direct confrontation with evil. He is an attractive and sympathetic figure, at once athletic, intelligent, and vulnerable. He suffers the doubts symptomatic of the modern age; his struggle with faith, his confusion, is ours. Two early scenes in the movie reveal his trials and the fault lines in his character. In the first, he begs for reassignment to New York, where he might care for his aging mother. He also voices concerns about whether he is fit to continue as a psychologist for priests. He confesses, "I think I've lost my faith." In the second, on one of his trips to New York, his uncle accusingly states, "if you weren't a priest, you'd be a famous psychiatrist and your mother" would not be destitute. As the pressure builds, we are shown a scene of Karras, the former boxer, pummeling a boxing dummy. This foreshadows the final scene of the film, where Karras will once again resort to pugilism to release his frustrations. The film accentuates male figures, especially priests and fathers, both by their presence and their absence. Questions about male authority and fidelity and about the nature of masculinity, courage, and violence are never far from the surface of the plot.

If Karras leads us into the action, he is not the principal opponent of the demon. The film begins with Father Merrin, a frail, elderly Jesuit and an experienced exorcist, on an archeological dig in Iraq, near the ancient biblical city of

Nineveh. When he discovers a small statue of a demon, he begins to tremble and makes plans at once to return to the United States. The opening foreshadows the ultimate explanation of the mysterious events now beginning in Georgetown. It also links the modern, skeptical world of contemporary America with the primitive and apparently superstitious world of the Middle East.

Merrin enters the house to the screeching sounds of the demon echoing his name through the building; he wants to begin the exorcism at once. Karras asks: "Do you want to hear the background of the case?" Merrin responds: "Why?" When Karras continues and notes that there seem to be three personalities, Merrin responds curtly: "There is only one."

The invading spirit seems less interested in Regan, an easy conquest, than in the priests. When Karras first visits Regan, the demon challenges him by saying, "The sow is mine." When Karras suggests an exorcism, the demon welcomes it as a means of bringing them closer together. Karras asks: "You and Regan?" The demon responds: "No. You and us." The spirit preys upon Karras's weaknesses, his faltering faith, and his guilt over abandoning his mother. Worn down by the rigors of the exorcism and especially by the devil's use of his now dead mother's voice to play upon his guilt, Karras is unable to continue. In the final scene, Merrin orders an exhausted and nearly defeated Karras to leave the room. When he returns, Karras discovers Merrin dead on the floor and the possessed child chuckling on the bed. He seizes Regan and beats her. When he realizes what he is doing, he stops and shouts, "take me." As the devil enters him, he strains to resist and then leans toward Regan as if to strangle her. Momentarily regaining control of himself, he hurls himself out the window and down the steps, where he lies limp and dying at the bottom. His closest friend, a Jesuit, arrives, holds Karras's hand and asks whether he is sorry for his sins. Karras flexes his hand in affirmation.

In his responses to critics, Blatty insisted that the film asserts the ultimate victory of goodness. So troubled were he and Friedkin about the ending that they added the scene of Karras willingly receiving absolution. Even so, ambiguities remain. The reality and efficacy of faith are not terribly prominent at the end. Merrin is undaunted, but given the lack of complexity of his character and the limited time he spends on screen, the audience has little connection with him. Chris MacNeil, the unbeliever most consciously affected by the possession, remains an unbeliever. She never sees the exorcism as anything more than a magical antidote to the inexplicable force controlling her daughter. So it seems that Karras, the troubled but sympathetic priest, is left to point us in the direction of the vindication of faith and goodness. His attack of Regan, which many audiences enthusiastically cheered, shows his flawed humanity. But it is also an act of doubt and despair. Nonetheless, his final act of self-sacrifice hints at a potential victory of love over hatred.

What *The Exorcist* wants to convey, but cannot quite, is that there is an intimate link of everyday vices and foibles to a cosmic battle between good and evil. Through our manifold weaknesses, we are vulnerable to assault from malevolent spiritual forces. If there is a way to overcome this danger, it points beyond morality narrowly construed to a narrative of redemption, not to what we achieve on our own, but to what can be done for us through a divine gift. The key to the battle between the devil and Merrin is that the latter is merely an instrument, admittedly a conscious and willing instrument, of the grace of Christ. This is one reason that the exorcist must adhere so closely to the prescribed ritual. The incarnation of evil in an act of possession is countered by the sensible signs of priestly vestments, scriptural prayers, and holy water, all of which reflect the incarnation of God himself in Christ. The sacramental response to evil requires free, human cooperation with the divine and the mediation of God's love and mercy through bodily things.

Without the prescribed ritual or some other means of expressing the love of God for the child, what little intelligibility there is to the human cooperation with the divine in the eradication of evil is lost. Indeed, except for the occasional maternal lamentations of Chris MacNeil, no one in the film expresses love for Regan. Even Merrin seems more interested in confronting his old nemesis than in restoring Regan to health. On the question of the purpose of possession an important exchange occurs in the book, only a severely truncated version of which made it into the movie:

> "Then what would be the purpose of possession?" Karras said, frowning. "What's the point?"
>
> "Who can know?" answered Merrin. "Who can really hope to know?" He thought for a moment. And then probingly continued: "Yet I think the demon's target is not the possessed. It's us . . . the observers. . . every person in this house. And I think—I think the point is to make us despair; to reject our own humanity, Damien: to see ourselves as ultimately bestial; as ultimately vile and putrescent; without dignity; ugly; unworthy."

The inclusion of this exchange would perhaps have

helped the audience not only to see more clearly what the devil intends, but also to make the transition from Karras to Merrin more smoothly. Even so, these are only words, and they pale by comparison with the transformation and degradation of Regan's body—her bloated, bruised, and distorted face, her projectile vomiting, her sinister, masculine voice—a spectacle that leaves the most lasting impression on the audience. The most repulsive scene in the entire film, in which Regan masturbates with a crucifix, foreshadows what will become a commonplace in later films: the treatment of sex as inherently vile and as indistinguishable from violence. The deepest problem with the film is that it is itself fascinated with the bestial, vile, and putrescent, and may lead us to see humanity as without dignity, ugly, and unworthy. By piling one shocking and destructive confrontation upon another, the ending risks granting the dramatic victory to the aesthetics of violence. The sacramental remedy would counter the view of the body as vile with the exaltation of lowly, infirm bodily things as signs and symbols of divine love and mercy.

The world of *The Exorcist* is one where ultimate justice is elusive, where we are tempted to see the underlying force as malevolent and punitive. There is a striking disproportion between the human longing for justice and mercy and the possibility of satisfaction. The film thus hints at a possibility, exploited fully in later films, of seeing violence and ineradicable guilt as the underlying truth about the human condition. Yet *The Exorcist* remains redolent with suggestions about evil and redemption precisely because it contains a multiplicity of perspectives and refuses the simplicity of a demonic monologue.

THE AESTHETICS OF EVIL

The consequences of reducing multiple perspectives to that of the demonic antihero are played out in two popular films from 1991, *Cape Fear* and *Silence of the Lambs*. These films, especially the former, treat the traditional divisions of good and evil and victims and assailants as mere conventions. Societal norms of right and wrong are obstacles to self-knowledge, obstacles that render us timid conformists. By contrast, anyone who breaks through the conventions attains a kind of clarity and resolve that most lack. If timidity is allied to conformity, courage manifests itself in creativity, in an artistic violation of the traditional codes of decent, law-abiding human beings. The political problem of courage—the difficulty of finding a place for it in a modern, bureaucratic society—gives rise to the antihero, admired for his antipolitical exercise of artistic boldness. Once these tendencies are unleashed, we are well on the way toward having sympathy for the devil.

The problem with the anti-hero's approach is that it undermines the gravity of the quest for evil. The seriousness of evil dissipates and the tone becomes one of satire or black comedy. Its sensationalistic scenes made *The Exorcist* a common target of satire on late-night comedy shows for years after its release; so too with the characters played by Robert DeNiro and Anthony Hopkins in *Cape Fear* and *Silence of the Lambs*. Where God is no longer a serious player, the devil's rebellion risks becoming comic. The antics of the demonic agent take center stage as the struggle between vice and virtue in the souls of ordinary people gradually recedes from view.

Cape Fear

In *Cape Fear*, Robert DeNiro plays an ex-convict, Cady, who returns from jail to torment his defense lawyer, played by Nick Nolte, whom he blames for his incarceration. *Cape Fear* is instructive not just because it contains themes germane to this study or because it explicitly links those themes to Nietzsche's philosophy, but also because it is a remake of a 1962 film of the same title. A comparison of the two versions is illuminating.

In the earlier film, often loosely associated with the genre of film *noir*, the distinction of good and evil seems clear from the very beginning. We first see Cady, the ex-convict played by Robert Mitchum, entering a courthouse. As he walks up the steps, he passes a woman carrying a stack of books. She drops one, but he never even notices her. This relatively minor act of incivility clues us in to his character. He has come to town to terrorize Sam Bowden, a lawyer, played by Gregory Peck, who had a confrontation with Cady eight years previously while on a visit to Baltimore. Bowden had heard a girl whimpering in an alley, gone to lend assistance, and scuffled with Cady. Since Bowden testified against him, Cady holds him responsible for his incarceration. While Peck does not play a hero, he is a respected member of his community, a faithful husband, and a good father. His wife and daughter are also reasonably intelligent, decent persons. There is not a hint of the detached, mocking tone of irony in the depiction of the Bowdens as upstanding American citizens.

The absence of irony does not mean that the American system of justice is beyond question, since it cannot provide complete protection from the likes of Cady. In spite of Bowden's close association with the police and their willingness to help, American law proves inadequate. The sense of helplessness of law-abiding citizens generates much of the fear in the story. In a pivotal scene, Bowden's wife makes the innocent mistake of leaving their daughter alone in the car for a few minutes while she attends to some errands. As Cady slowly and deliberately approaches the car, the girl panics and escapes into an adjacent building. When she hears footsteps pursuing her, she runs out of the building and into the street where she is struck by a car. She is unhurt, but the encounter reinforces the sense of the Bowdens' vulnerability to Cady's threat.

Cady's brutality is most explicitly brought out when he takes a woman he has just met to a hotel for sex. Once in the room, the mood turns ominous. The woman lies in the bed facing Cady who stands at its foot. She reads the harmful intent in his eyes, cowers in fear, and makes a futile attempt to escape. When next we meet her, she is beaten, distraught, ashamed, and so fearful of retaliation that she is unwilling to press charges against Cady even when Bowden tells her of the threat to his daughter. Bowden reluctantly looks beyond the law for help, first from a private investigator and then, at the investigator's suggestion, from some thugs who attempt to rough Cady up. When all else fails and an attack on their daughter is imminent, the Bowdens begin to plot a way to lure Cady into a situation where he can be caught or killed.

The sense of being caught in a labyrinth, the accent on the limits to law, and the temptation of the victim to embrace evil—these are all motifs of film *noir*. The Bowdens come gradually to the unsettling realization that they cannot rely exclusively on the law, that they will have to exercise ingenuity in their battle with evil. They decide to take matters into their own hands, initially by attempting to intimidate Cady, and then by setting a trap for him. At this juncture, it is not so clear who is on the side of the law. Situated now somewhere between the law and Cady, the Bowdens put their own character in question and risk being seduced by Cady's nihilism.

Significantly, the climactic scene in *Cape Fear* occurs on a houseboat outside the city. The return from the man-made world of the city to the natural world allows for two possible resolutions. The first is the nihilistic discovery that there is no natural basis for the American system of justice—that might makes right. The second is the recognition of a natural standard more fundamental than, but finally compatible with, conventional law. The Bowdens' ruse is not a path away from conventional justice but a circuitous route to its confirmation. When Bowden finally has Cady in a position where Bowden could kill him, he exercises restraint and chooses instead to let him rot in prison where he can contemplate his failed attempt at vengeance. The concluding note is thus one of a sober and modest justification of the American system, of the need for the procedures of justice to be complemented by virtues of prudence, loyalty, courage, and restraint. Though Bowden's entire family exercises courage, their virtue is allied to a host of others and is never celebrated as an end in itself. By contrast, Cady's unrestrained boldness is but a simulacrum of real courage, and his preying upon innocent women and children reveal him to be unmanly and cowardly.

Almost thirty years later, in 1991, Martin Scorsese directed a new version of *Cape Fear*. In giving small parts to

Mitchum and Peck, Scorsese clearly reveals he has the previous version in mind. He hints at the contrast between the two versions by shifting the two actors' allegiances. Mitchum now plays a detective attempting to catch Cady, while Peck is the sleazy lawyer defending Cady. No character in the later version of the film is admirable. When we first meet Bowden, played by Nick Nolte, he is on the verge of an affair with a colleague. We soon learn that his past infidelities have nearly ruined his marriage. When the latest object of his lust is beaten and raped by Cady, Bowden shows little or no remorse, even after she confesses to him that she ended up with Cady because Bowden had stood her up. Bowden's relationship to Cady is likewise not without ambiguity. Fourteen years previously, he had defended Cady in a rape case and, because of the brutality of the act, had suppressed a report that the victim was promiscuous.

The most striking contrast between the two versions is in the depiction of the Bowden family. A not-so-subtle mixture of sensuality and violence underlies their lives. The daughter, who has suffered from the indifference and hostility of her parents toward one another, is withdrawn and inarticulate, with pathetically little sense of self. After she gets in trouble at school for smoking marijuana, her father yells at her, but confides privately to his wife that it is not such a big deal—it is almost a sacrament in some societies—to which she responds, "Yeah, along with incest, necrophilia, and bestiality." This is the family produced by liberal individualism and its sexual revolution. Composed of isolated individuals dominated by their private lusts, this is a family based not on trust and mutual affection but on lies and suspicion. Their interaction is characterized by a studied avoidance and accusing silence, broken by explosive verbal assaults and recriminations. The Bowdens have nothing of substance to hand on to their child. Their barely suppressed violence is the natural result of their futile attempt to retain traditional marital roles in a nihilistic culture. Even more than in *The Exorcist*, in *Cape Fear* the disorder in the family anticipates the evil to be wrought by the assailant.

Bowden's wife, played by Jessica Lange, is especially amoral. She alternates between being horrified at Cady's acts and wishing for further confrontations. After Cady kills their dog, she weeps but quickly recovers to shout, "I'd . . . like to kill him." As in the earlier version, the Bowdens attempt to set up Cady. As they wait for him, she calmly admits to Bowden: "I'd like to know how strong we are or how weak." The only way to do that, she adds, is by confronting Cady. She is well ahead of her husband, at least in her willingness to match violence with violence. Bowden, although accustomed to a host of vices, confesses to the private investigator that he does not know whether he can "live with killing a man," and the final scene of the movie finds him writhing in horror at the blood on his hands.

In *Cape Fear*, the only example of a common bond between characters occurs when Cady, pretending to be Bowden's daughter's new drama teacher, calls her on the telephone to introduce himself and set up a meeting with her. Both over the phone and face to face, he plays upon her disaffection from her parents, upon her teenage sense of being misunderstood, and upon her emerging sense of her own sexuality. Even after she becomes suspicious and realizes who he is, he allays her fears by playing upon her hunger for understanding and affection. Predictably, she sympathizes with him. Where does this leave the audience?

The feelings of sympathy for the victims soon turn to

repulsion—or worse, to a kind of detached enjoyment at the spectacle of evil. Recall Scorsese's comment that it is a story about a guy who wants revenge and it is a lot of fun. The only positive feeling that one can take away from a film like the Scorsese *Cape Fear* is a macho feeling of achievement at having endured so much terror. Is this not precisely the education that the pseudo-Nietzschean Cady offers? We participate in his exhilarating project of surpassing established limits and overcoming prohibitions. If law and morality no longer educate or reform, they do serve to heighten and intensify the pleasure derived from acts of violation. The explicit and excessive reliance on sensationalist gore in the newer version of *Cape Fear* overwhelms the imagination and stupefies the intellect. It exercises a tyranny over the imagination that resembles Cady's control over the bodies of his victims. (By contrast, the older version of *Cape Fear* hints at violence by presenting it partially or indirectly.) Gone are *The Exorcist*'s attention to subtle differences in character and multiple perspectives on the human condition. These are replaced by a superficial aesthetics of evil, by trying to outdo other films in the depiction of offensive and degrading acts. This competition is subject to the law of diminishing returns. Once a film has deployed nearly all the available means of explicit terror, it is difficult to surpass it.

Whatever depth there is in the recent *Cape Fear* is derivative of its overt philosophical nihilism. Both movies depict Cady as having received something of a legal education in jail, but only the Scorsese version invests him with philosophical significance. We learn from the investigator who is tailing him that he spent part of a day in a library reading Nietzsche's *Thus Spake Zarathustra*. Both the investigator and Bowden know that Nietzsche said "God is dead," but they do not comment on the central role of the superman in *Zarathustra*. Cady fancies himself a Nietzschean superman. After he beats back the attackers hired by Bowden to rough him up, he yells that he can out-think them, out-philosophize them, and out-fight them. Quoting an obscure seventeenth-century philosopher, he adds that God is not above him nor he beneath him. His "mission" in jail was to "become more than human." The criminal justice system has failed miserably to educate Cady in the social virtues of American society, whatever they might be. In the absence of any clearly defined sense of the virtues to which American life is ordered or of a persuasive vision of the goals of our society, the procedures of the justice system are but thinly veiled instruments of illegitimate coercion. Jail taught Cady that power is arbitrary and that whatever deprivation and punishment one is subjected to can be put to good use. So prison made him stronger and less vulnerable, more capable of evil and less susceptible to the pull of a social conscience. He is liberated from the code of good and evil that society through both covert and overt means impresses on the memory of its citizens. He is beyond good and evil.

On the surface at least, these are all Nietzschean themes. For Nietzsche, man is the as yet undetermined animal, an animal that creates its own values and whose future leaders will engage in acts of self-overcoming to bring about a revaluation of all values. Such a project entails, first, seeing through the conventional code of morality operative in one's society and, second, a violent destruction of that code in order to clear a path for new and more vital ways of life.

At the end of the film, we are left not only with little clarification concerning the distinction between good and evil, but also with the question whether either side has won. This version also ends at Cape Fear, outside the city and back to nature. But the coastal resort is under siege from a torrential storm. Mirroring the tumult in Cady's soul, nature itself is a merciless vortex of destruction. After a seemingly endless series of confrontations with Cady on his boat, Bowden manages to handcuff Cady to the boat. As it is torn apart by the raging water, Bowden's wife and daughter are thrown free. Nearly at the shoreline, Bowden and Cady beat each other with rocks. Finally, the tide pulls Cady into and eventually under the water. As he sinks, Cady laughs and then sings, "I'm bound for the promised land." In this final act, which denies any possibility of rectification or justice, Cady affirms his own way of life. His clarity of purpose surpasses that of all the other characters, immersed as they are in their bourgeois world of petty pleasures, socially acceptable vices, and suppressed violence.

In contrast to the previous version, in the later movie Cady is not the antithesis of society but its liberation from weak traditions of law and order. He is not a coward whose recourse to violence against the innocent and the weak is symptomatic of his wickedness, but rather one who sees that, since all are implicated in evil, no one is innocent. He comprehends and transcends the social world of weak souls who need one another and the law to reinforce their petty view that self-restraint is good and strength, wicked. In Nietzschean language, the basis of this social world is resentment at those who distinguish themselves as individuals, who exhibit a courageous self-affirmation and refuse to conform to the opinions of the majority.

Is Cady, then, an incarnation of Nietzsche's superman, of his anti-Christ? Nietzsche describes his "free spirit" as being educated by "everything evil, terrible and tyrannical in man." He feels "malice against the lures of dependence that lie hidden in honors, or money, or offices."[2] Cady practices the virtue of courage, of heroic individualism, the virtue most lacking in modern society. Like Nietzsche, he is obsessed with Christianity, with tattoos of biblical texts decorating his body. Despite these similarities, Cady is not a neat fit with Nietzsche's superman. He promotes making strength out of fear and is motivated by resentment and revenge, the motives not of Nietzsche's superman but of the petty and sickly soul of the slave. His destructive tendencies are ordered to no great re-creation of higher ideals. His crude and uncomprehending recitation of fragments of a philosophy of the superman are precisely what result from a popularization of Nietzsche's teaching, from the confused attempt of the lower type of soul to live out the destiny of the higher type. He is not, then, beyond the bourgeois Christian world but merely its mirror image. Although Nietzsche would certainly find Cady's character wanting, even comical, his criticisms would not be those commonly associated with traditional morality. If Nietzsche's project was to induce a state of chaos into society to incite a search for new modes of life, then he could have little objection to Cady, except to say that neither Cady nor Scorsese should be confused with artists of the highest rank.

Silence of the Lambs

Cape Fear was not the most important or successful movie of 1991 to address the topic of evil. That year the Oscar for best picture went to *Silence of the Lambs*, as did the awards for best actor and actress. Since the plot was rather flimsy, the best picture award might be seen as a second commendation of Anthony Hopkins, whose portrayal of the cannibalistic serial killer, Hannibal Lecter, was the film's great draw. Closer to Nietzsche in his refined aesthetic sense, Hopkins's Hannibal shares with DeNiro's Cady a penchant for the aesthetics of evil. As in *The Exorcist*, in *Silence* the authority of medical and psychiatric science comes under relentless scrutiny. Since Lecter himself is the most talented psychiatrist we encounter in the film and rejects science's ability to interpret *him*, we are continually confronted with science's shortcomings. *Silence* also brings evil into closer alignment with the judicial system.

The movie begins with Clarise Starling, an FBI trainee played by Jodie Foster, invited to participate in the investigation of a serial murder case. The murderer has been given the nickname Buffalo Bill because he peels off the hides of his victims. Early on, Starling's superior sends her to interview Lecter, a highly successful psychiatrist turned cannibalistic murderer, now housed in a psychiatric prison in Baltimore. Starling thinks she is simply there to get information about Lecter when in fact her superior hopes that, having developed a rapport with Lecter, she will be able to elicit from him a case analysis of Buffalo Bill.

A salient but mysterious clue in the Buffalo Bill murders is the presence of a butterfly in the mouths of the victims. Lecter interprets this as a symbol of the killer's quest for self-transformation. Starling hits upon a likely behaviorist interpretation: the killer is a transvestite. Lecter counters that the killer only thinks he is a transvestite. Underlying the sexual deviancy is a deeper longing for a transformation of a different sort. Into what, we are never told—perhaps into the sort of being Lecter has become? But we do learn that violence, murder, and sexual perversion are the instruments of artistic self-fashioning, an art exercised with clinical detachment on the bodies of victims.

Lecter takes the criminal's understanding of himself as beyond good and evil to its logical conclusion, turning evil into high art. His sense of decorum is evident in his assertion that "discourtesy is unspeakably ugly." After Lecter makes his escape, Clarise is confident he will not come after her: "I can't explain it. He would consider that rude." Lecter is learned, even something of a philosopher. He counsels Clarise to return to first principles and to follow the advice of Marcus Aurelius, who stipulated that of each thing you must ask, "what is it in itself? . . .what is its nature?" But his refinement exists alongside, or better coincides with, an unspeakable brutality. The point is dramatically brought out in the pivotal scene near the end of the film, when Lecter escapes by viciously murdering two armed police guards. As he completes his task, his face covered with the blood of his victims, he deftly wields an officer's nightstick in the manner of a conductor. His musical accompaniment? Bach's *Goldberg Variations*.

In exchange for information on the Buffalo Bill case, Lecter demands that Starling answer questions about her own life. One of the conversations between Starling and Lecter unveils the motives behind her choice of profession. After relating her worst childhood memory, the death of her father, Clarise tells how, as an orphan, she was sent to live on a ranch, where she awakened one morning to a horrifying sound. Upon investigation, she discovered lambs screaming as they were being slaughtered. She opened the gate for the lambs but none escaped. In a vain attempt to save at least one of them, she grabbed a lamb and ran away.

She was, of course, found, and the lamb was killed. As Lecter proceeds with his analysis, Clarise admits that the screaming of the lambs still haunts her dreams. Lecter concludes that she is pursuing the serial killer in the hope of silencing the lambs by saving an innocent victim. The importance of Starling's confession is manifold. It provides us with her motive: to save the innocent. It also implicitly raises the question at the heart of the old problem of evil: What sort of universe allows for the capricious slaying of the innocent? Both Lecter's resistance to psychological explanation and Starling's motives force us to confront the reality of evil and the unanswerable questions it raises. These themes help to explain Lecter's willingness to work with her, even though his choice is by no means a moral judgment. Instead, it reflects his aesthetics: Starling is more authentic, less trapped in the categories of behaviorism than are the other authorities.

But Clarise does not finally provide a viable alternative to either of the two dominant worldviews in the story, that of bureaucratic, behaviorist law-enforcement and Lecter's aesthetization of evil. She is Lecter's student, a supposition reinforced by the similarity between his name and the Latin word *lector*, which literally means reader but has connotations of one who instructs by lecturing. His name also calls to mind the term "lecher" (in French, the word *lechier* means to lick). While he has a sense of decorum, his instruction of Clarise is akin to a sexual possession of her. The crucial clue about Buffalo Bill, the one that leads Clarise directly to him, is that, in Hannibal's words, he "covets." What do we covet? What we see every day. The clue leads Clarise back to the town of the first victim, since the killer must have begun by coveting what he saw in the neighborhood where he lived.

From the start, Lecter covets Clarise. In their first encounter he silently gazes upon her, looking her up and down. A *lector* or reader is someone who interprets by looking or gazing. His psychoanalysis of the deepest secrets of her life is also a kind of covetousness, arising out of a desire to gaze upon, and exploit for his own pleasure, the precious secrets of her psyche. In order to gain what she wants from him, Clarise agrees to Lecter's demand of a *quid pro quo* and thus willingly submits to his use of her life for his own pleasure. Whatever may be its practical efficacy, her consenting to his game subordinates her own vision of the world to his.

Precisely because it is combined with such a sense of decorum and erudition, Lecter's evil is more frightening and more baffling than that of a typical serial killer. Lecter's aesthetization of evil is in part a protest against the standard analyses of evil in his own profession. He refuses to conform to any behaviorist mold. In his first meeting with Starling, she feebly attempts to capitalize on his initial willingness to talk by suggesting that he fill out a questionnaire she has brought along. Lecter balks: "A census taker once tried to test me. I ate his liver with some fava beans and a fine chianti." He refuses to degrade himself by becoming an instrument; he retains what Nietzsche calls the "pathos of distance" separating the high from the mediocre. In the world of behaviorist psychology, where everything can be explained by case studies and statistics, by tracing deviancy to some causal root in the patient's history, there is no freedom and no evil. Lecter's successful attempt at eluding the neat categories of psychiatry is a twisted assertion of the reality of freedom, of evil, and of his superiority to those around him. What behaviorism overlooks is what Nietzsche calls the "basic fact" of the human condition, the "human will . . . which needs a goal—and it will rather will nothingness than not will."[3] The willing of destruction, of annihilation, as an end in itself is a response to the attempt to eliminate inequality, distinction, and freedom from human life.

Given the modern scientific understanding of human behavior in terms of natural laws, everything is determined by chemical reactions and evil arises solely from a miscalculation of the appropriate way of satisfying genetically determined inclinations. This is the philosophy of progress; anyone who demurs is labeled irrational and sent for medical treatment. If one actually tries to live consciously in accord with Enlightenment dicta, the result is a paralyzing hyperconsciousness, psychic inertia. (The classic statement of this is Dostoevsky's *Notes from the Underground*.) Precisely what is supposed to lead to the rational satisfaction of all our longings deprives our deliberations of meaning and our actions of any root in freedom. Having seen the presuppositions and consequences of Enlightenment theory, who could go on as before? Indeed, who could act at all? If this is right, then there is the possibility of immersing oneself in evil precisely as a means of asserting one's freedom and dignity. This is Lecter's path.

Lecter's cannibalism is the antithesis of civilization, which always includes a code protecting the innocent and requiring hospitality to strangers. In ancient societies, it was a mark of humanity to see oneself in the position of the stranger, in his position of weakness and dependency. Hannibal's cannibalism, his incorporating others into himself like food, is a most emphatic denial of the otherness and independence of persons. It is an affront not only to ancient codes of hospitality but also and more pointedly to our code of inalienable human rights and individual dignity. He feeds on other humans (making exceptions not for the innocent but for those he deems "interesting") the way we feed on lower animals. Once again, the body is a vile thing, a putrid object. This is true, whether in the FBI laboratory's analyses of the corpses or in Buffalo Bill's collection of human hides, or, most dramatically, in Hannibal's cannibalism. Modern psychology is perfectly free to analyze him as suffering from an acute, narcissistic personality disorder, just as he is free to dismiss that analysis as an attempt to explain his evil away rather than to account for it. Indeed, since there is a comical disproportion between the purported cause and the effect, Lecter will certainly have the last laugh and the last happy meal.

Equality and dignity, the founding principles of Enlightenment politics, are precisely the source of the problem in the behaviorist world of the American criminal justice system. In that world, we are all case studies, reducible to the influences of nature and nurture on us. Everything is predetermined by our past; the future is already a closed book. The only way to excel, to exhibit one's individuality in such a world—a world that has so debased its moral language that goodness is equated with normalcy, that is, with routine conformity—is to violate conventions in ways that transcend the standard categories deployed to explain and hence control the abnormal. Lecter exploits the tensions between our hyperbolic rhetoric of individual choice and self-expression, on the one hand, and our sense of increasing homogenization and uniformity, on the other.

Given the evanescence of supernatural, natural, and conventional codes of conduct, traditional heroism is no longer possible, and *Silence* in the end celebrates Lecter as antihero. The entire FBI psychiatric team is dependent upon

Hannibal's insight. Surrounded by subhumans, he is super-human: nearly omniscient, he is able to read the secrets of souls on the basis of the slightest hints; virtually omnipotent, he is endowed not so much with physical strength as with supreme cunning and adroitness. At the end, Lecter calls Clarise from the Bahamas. He congratulates her on capturing Buffalo Bill, asks whether the lambs have quit crying, and assures her that he will not trouble her. As she inquires about his plans, the camera shifts from Lecter to Dr. Frederick Chilton, Lecter's nemesis at the Baltimore psychiatric prison. Lecter tells Clarice he is having an old friend for dinner. His insouciant manner of expressing his anticipation of Chilton's murder gives a comical note to the ending. The audience is transported from the world of Clarise who has sympathy for victims to that of Lecter who eats them. There are no grounds for seeing Hannibal as tragic. But if we find him comic, do we not have a kind of sympathy for the devil? Sympathy here no longer means pity, since that emotion has been jettisoned along with traditional morality. Instead, it means that we have shifted our way of seeing the world, so that we now see it from the devil's perspective and share his comic take on the bankruptcy of all moral codes.

The comic trajectory of much of contemporary horror presupposes that we have found something attractive in the malignant hero, something that seduces us. His theatrics demolish the Enlightenment assumption of the neutral observer. Just as Cady and Lecter implicate their interlocutors in their own "liberating" perversity, so too the crafters of their stories implicate us in their visions. The danger is that our laughter will be but an echo of the cynical, mocking laughter of the invading spirit in *The Exorcist*. Of course, the immediate effect of the laughter is the welcome feeling of being released from terror. But even this sort of laughter cancels the great quest for evil by divesting it of significance.

The problem with these heroes is that they negate much but affirm nothing. In his perceptive study of popular culture, Mark Edmundson describes a dialectical opposition between Gothic elements and the strategy of "facile transcendence." The Gothic celebrates hero-villains and depicts all of life as haunted. The dominant, contemporary "antidote" to the Gothic is what Edmundson calls "facile transcendence."[4] It portrays reality in neat and tidy terms and dismisses sinister evil as the stuff of overactive, adolescent imaginations. As Edmundson hints, our Gothic is itself rather facile. Our would-be anti-heroes and "avenging angels" have no depth; they are all surface. While they toy with the gap between appearance and reality, they simply substitute the artistic appearances of terror for the appearances of conventional society. Once we see this, they lose their tragic gravity and become comic figures. If the genre of facile transcendence opts for a simplistic metaphysics of goodness, the genre of the debased Gothic opts for a crude and literal metaphysics of evil. If evil is all there is, there is ultimately nothing.

The question is: Where do we go from here? What is the next step in the dramatic depiction of evil? The most obvious move is simply to continue along the same path and to increase the quantity and quality of offensive and shocking material. But this becomes tiresome or ludicrous, as the attempted manipulation of the audience must resort to ever more preposterous methods. Instead of an intimidating profundity, there is a shallowness to the presentation of evil. Evil becomes, in Hannah Arendt's apt term, banal. What makes up for the lack of depth is increasing aesthetic complexity on the surface of the action. As both artist and audience become less capable of taking evil seriously, the adoption of a comic perspective on evil is quite natural. To the topic of the banality of evil—what one critic nicely describes as the "comic beat of never-ending terror"—we will turn in the next chapter. Before we do so, however, we need to look at two less predictable responses to the current problem of evil, *L.A. Confidential* (1997) and *Seven* (1996), both of which have been labelled neo-*noir*.

THE RECOVERY OF FILM *Noir*

L.A. Confidential

L.A. Confidential is different from the other productions we have considered in this chapter. It contains no super-human criminal and and no dialectical opposition between the liberating grandeur of demonic evil and conventional mores. It returns us to evil on a human scale; the range of the characters and the different, if complementary, internal battles they wage reflect the diversity of human types. By the end of the film, the flaws in each of these characters will be painfully revealed. The labyrinthine plot of the film is itself a trial of character; it imposes upon individuals a realization of their own limitations and their dependence on others. The accentuation of the limits of human character—the way weaknesses leave us prey to our own blindness and to the malice of others—is a standard lesson of film *noir*. And *L.A. Confidential* is the most impressive recent installment in that genre, largely because it successfully revivifies American life in the 1950s, close to the era of film *noir*.

What makes *L.A. Confidential* pertinent is its sophisticated depiction of the aesthetics of evil. The gap between appearance and reality pervades the story, tempting us to conclude that reality is nothing but perception, that the world has no substance but is rather a series of competing appearances. As the opening credits roll and we are treated to postcard images of Los Angeles and its domestic tranquility, a voice-over intones: "Life is good in L.A.: it's paradise on earth . . . but there's trouble in paradise." The voice is that of Danny DeVito's Sid Hudgens, the scandal-mongering editor of the tabloid *Hush Hush*. As always in this genre, paradise, in the form of a beautiful woman, is another source of deception. The seductive, street-smart, and morally compromised female lead, obligatory in a *noir*, is Lynn, played by Kim Basinger. A Veronica Lake look-alike, Lynn works for Pierce Pachett, a millionaire pimp, who has his women "cut" to look like movie stars in order to service the fantasies of his affluent and influential clients. The suggestion that art satisfies our ideals only after it has first constructed those ideals by falsifying reality extends beyond the realm of *eros* or beauty to the realm of justice. Of the four policemen who figure prominently in the film, the most celebrated is the opportunistic Jack Vincennes (Kevin Spacey), the adviser to a television series, *Badge of Honor*, whose platitudes and tidy plots paint a comforting picture of American justice. Behind the scenes, Jack is on the *Hush Hush* payroll, working with Sid to stage photographed arrests.

The three other crime-fighting principals are Bud White, Ed Exley, and Dudley Smith. Bud is the brawling bad cop, the department's interrogating instrument of terror, who is willing to beat confessions out of suspects, plant evidence on them, or summarily execute them. His only admirable trait is his chivalry; his ire is especially piqued by men who abuse defenseless women. Ed Exley is the young, uncompromising voice of justice, whose father was killed in the line of duty by an unknown assailant. This, we learn later, was Ed's original motive in becoming a cop: to catch the guys who think they can get away with it. Almost from the outset, however, we are led to be suspicious of Ed's moralism, chiefly becuase he is so smug and ambitious. Dudley Smith, colleague of Ed's father, is the cynical captain, who uses Bud's brutality wherever it serves him and chastises Ed for his unwillingness to adopt the principle that the end justifies the means. But it is not just Dudley's use of means that is questionable. It will turn out that he is allied with Patchett to control organized crime in the city of angels. Void of conscience and human attachment, he has the clarity of purpose of the truly malicious.

What appears to be a straightforward unmasking of American life in the 1950s is something much more interesting and complex. The gap between appearance and reality is a vehicle not only for undermining the cover story but also for the possibility of positive change and development on the part of characters. They can be deceived about themselves and others, about what they want, and what they are willing to do to get it. These characters are not static; they only seem to be trapped in their illusions. Self-doubt opens up the possibility of recovering a conviction of who they really are, a suggestion of direction and purpose to their lives.

What pushes the characters into crises of self-confidence are the conflicts in the plot which revolves around two crimes. On Christmas Eve, the youthful Ed, who is nominally in charge of the precinct for the evening, poses for photographs and jokes with reporters who are writing a human-interest story entitled "Silent Night with the LAPD." But the mood changes rapidly as reports surface that fellow officers have been beaten, and a group of Mexicans are brought in as suspects. Angry cops brush Ed aside and proceed to take out their frustrations on the Mexicans. When the reporters spread photographs of the melee across the front page of the paper under the title "Bloody Christmas," the department is caught in a public relations nightmare. In the ensuing inquiry, Ed orchestrates his own elevation to detective-lieutenant and the demotion of Bud White and Jack Vincennes. In a subsequent case, involving the slaying of six people at the Nite Owl diner, including an ex-policeman and one of Patchett's cosmetically improved prostitutes, Ed plays the self-righteous hero. During two encounters with the suspects, all black, Ed and Bud kill them all. Apparently dominated by ambition and fame, Ed has now become the public image of the LAPD.

But neither he nor Bud is beyond hope of redemption. Both are plagued by doubts about whether the now-dead suspects were the real perpetrators. At this point Lynn becomes the pivotal character in the plot. She and Bud become romantically involved, but since she works for Patchett, her motives are unclear. Their relationship does reveal their better angels; they share a longing for communication, affection, and love. Their intimacy allows for expressions of vulnerability. Lynn's private bedroom, not the one she uses for paid sex, is decorated with reminders of her childhood in Brisbee, Arizona; Bud confesses to Lynn that he watched his father beat his mother to death. He voices doubts about whether he is smart enough to solve the Nite Owl case, but Lynn encourages him.

As Ed and Bud pursue their independent investigations

of the Nite Owl case, Dudley worries that they may uncover his own involvement. He enlists the aid of Sid and, through Patchett, Lynn to provide Bud with photographs of Ed and Lynn making love. Predictably enraged, Bud confronts Lynn and, in a replaying of his father's own misogyny, begins to beat her. Startled by this act, he retreats to find and pummel Ed, who actually fares better than one might have thought and eventually succeeds in persuading Bud that someone is trying to put them at odds with one another. They team up and begin to unravel the case. As they work together, White and Exley begin to take on one another's virtues. The physical Bud becomes more intelligent and more restrained. The naïve, moralistic, and effete Ed becomes tougher and more pragmatic.

Even the smooth Jack Vincennes has a change of heart. Before seeking Bud's assistance, Ed had already enlisted Jack's help. Jack, seemingly along just for the ride, has a change of heart after cooperating with Sid to set up a young, bisexual, would-be actor to be photographed in a compromising position with the gay district attorney. As his self-disgust mounts, Jack sits in a bar, looks up, and sees himself in a mirror. For the first time, he sees something more than the image of himself that he has been complicit in constructing with Sid, the master of image-making sleaze. He sets out to warn the actor but is too late. The man has been murdered. Jack's newfound pursuit of truth will soon prove his undoing. Rededicated to solving the Nite Owl case, Jack innocently solicits the help of Dudley, who kills him.

Not long before his conversion, Jack and Ed discuss why they became policemen. Ed describes the impact of his father's unsolved murder, but Jack mutters, "I can't remember." And yet he does remember, and we are left with the conviction that he was nobler in death and defeat than he ever was in life. At roughly the same time that this conversation occurs, Bud is also asking and answering the question why he became a cop. The suggestion is not that they can recover a pristine innocence of motive. Given the world they inhabit, innocence is a liability, as is excessive moral purity. But they can recover in an adult way something of their original thirst for justice.

In the film's finale, Bud and Ed are set up by Dudley at an abandoned, out-of-town hotel. In the shootout, Bud and Ed kill or gravely injure all the bad cops except Dudley. The exchange of gunfire leaves them both wounded; Bud's injuries, suffered when he risked his life to save Ed, are serious, perhaps fatal. As approaching sirens wail, Dudley and Exley emerge from the hotel. Dudley taunts Exley, "Are you going to shoot me or arrest me?" Ed opts for certain if questionable justice and shoots Dudley. In the aftermath, the department publishes a less than accurate version of events and is forced once again to make Exley its hero. After Ed receives his medal, Lynn greets him and leads him outside. Their exchange indicates that whatever progress Exley's character may have made, indeed whatever affirmation of justice the film may make, is tentative: "I tried to throw it all away and they gave it back in spades," Exley says. With a knowing smile, Lynn responds: "You couldn't resist." Exley smiles: "They're using me and for a little while I'm using them."

Lynn escorts Ed to a car where a heavily bandaged Bud waits. Ed thanks Bud for saving his life. Before driving off with Bud, Lynn kisses Ed and says, "Some men get the world. Others get ex-hookers and a trip to Arizona."

The moral amibiguity of the ending, which signals the uncertain future of Exley's relationship to the LAPD, qualifies without denying his development. *Eros*, it appears, has freed Lynn from her morally compromising life and Bud from the mechanical chain of violence he has inherited from his father. The final frames of the film show an episode of *Badge of Honor* being dedicated to Vincennes. The irony is that he finally earned it.

Seven

If *L.A. Confidential*'s *noir*ish authenticity rests largely on its historical detail, the commendation of *Seven*, with its contemporary urban setting, as a film *noir* is much less secure. And yet it succeeds in bringing the virtues of *noir* to bear upon what might otherwise be a standard serial-killer story. *Seven* pits Somerset, a seasoned, intelligent, somewhat jaded member of the New York City homicide department, and Mills, a young, brash, and mildly idealistic detective, against a serial killer whose motif is the seven deadly sins. While the film continues the narrative of the serial killer as anti-hero, whose explosive crimes are judgments on a corrupt society, it suggests other and richer possibilities for the construal of the nature and meaning of evil. If anything, this film is more chilling than the ones we have discussed thus far. Its response to the problem of the artistic presentation of evil in a nihilistic world is to reassert with a vengeance the primacy of the tragic construal of evil. By the use of clever and veiled artifice, it makes it impossible for the audience to adopt a detached, ironic point of view. More than the previous movies, this film attends to the development of character and especially to the question of why someone would fight against evil in a world where it seems invincible.

Adopting a standard strategy in detective stories, the film introduces the two main characters as polar opposites. It pairs a young, enthusiastic detective with an older, jaded mentor: Somerset is old, reflective, and nearly cynical, while Mills is young, idealistic, and emotional. Somerset drinks wine; Mills, beer. Somerset wants out and is in fact seven days from retirement when the first murder occurs. He is tired and describes his job as ineffectual, as just "picking up the pieces." He depicts poetically the seeming pointlessness of detective work and the elusiveness of justice: "So many corpses roll away unavenged." Yet his intellect is piqued by odd clues; once he glimpses the design of the latest serial killer, whom he describes as "methodical, exacting, and patient," he goes to the library to read texts like Dante's *Inferno* and Milton's *Paradise Lost*. In his study *Somewhere in the Night: Film* Noir *and the American City*, Nicholas Christopher notes that *Seven* mythically conflates New York and Hell. It is as if Dante's *Inferno* is a map of the city. Somerset never indulges in psychological speculation about the killer. Mills, by contrast, is naïve and brash. Thinking he might make a difference, he fought to get reassigned from upstate to the city. He thinks the killer is a lunatic and opts for Cliff's Notes over the poetry of Dante, whom he dismisses as a "poet faggot." The negative view of Mills as combative, ignorant, and cocky is tempered when his wife reveals to Somerset that she knew he was the one for her the day they met because he was the "funniest" guy she had ever known. He is also not without insight; he sees through Somerset's repeated claims of indifference and despair countering, "You don't believe this."

While Mills is most obviously engaged in a kind of contest with the killer (he unknowingly berates the killer who shows up at a murder scene disguised as a cameraman and is later nearly killed by him in a chase scene), the deeper parallels are between the killer and Somerset. He is the first to pick up on the clues and to trace them to the didactic medieval literature on sin, in which the punishment mirrors the crime. Somerset realizes early on that the tortures and murders have both a proximate and an ultimate goal. The former is "forced attrition," wherein one regrets one's sins but not because one loves God. The latter goal is the same as the didactic end of medieval sermons: to convert the world. Somerset's complaint that we "embrace and nurture apathy as if it were virtue" anticipates the killer's indictment of modern society. Somerset counters Mills's view (and the dominant American view, at least in the media) that freaks and nuts are responsible for evil with the observation that evil is an everyday occurrence, the stuff of ordinary life.

As they close in on the killer, they realize why he has been so difficult to trace. He shaves the skin off his fingers to avoid leaving fingerprints even in his own home, which he has turned into a cheesy, baroque Catholic religious shrine, full of crosses, bibles, and rosaries. In an act symbolic of his martyrdom, he has taken the name John Doe. Like Cady in the later version of *Cape Fear*, John Doe appears to suffer from a religious pathology. Were it not that other characters in the film share something of his appraisal of his victims, indeed of modern urban life, we might be inclined to think that his project is the result of his religious fanaticism, a fanaticism that generates excessively elevated and unrealistic standards for human behavior. The frustration at the failure of others and perhaps of themselves to meet these standards sometimes leads individuals to lash out at others. But this is not the appraisal the film leads us to make. Although the police hunt for the killer, they share his disgust at the lives of his victims. For example, when the victim accused of sloth, a drug-dealing pederast whom the killer has kept barely alive in his bed and tortured for a year, is brought to the hospital in a coma, the doctor first comments that the victim has "experienced as much pain and suffering" as a human being is capable of. He then adds, "He still has hell to look forward to." The detectives are repulsed by the vanity of another victim, a gorgeous model whom the killer cleverly tortures by cutting off her nose, tying her to her bed, and then gluing a telephone to one of her hands and a bottle of pills to the other. Unwilling to call for help, since that would mean living with her disfigurement, she commits suicide.

The film leads us to adopt the perspective of the killer in its presentation of the victims. We see them as the killer would have us see them. We see neither their torture and death nor the grieving of disconsolate relatives and friends. We see them only after they're dead and only through the lens of the killer's commentary on their lives, a commentary that argues for the fittingness of their punishment. The vile body becomes a means of instruction, as it is the site of punishment and a physical manifestation of the vices of the soul. The movie thus gives us maximum sympathy with the killer's perspective, with the theatrics of his morality play, lifted largely from Dante. John Doe is almost a high-brow version of the vigilante, made familiar in numerous Charles Bronson films. In contrast to those films, which are preoccupied with the question of the justification of vigilante methods, there is no real debate about John Doe's style of working outside the law. The American justice system is not so much corrupt as utterly powerless; reform is no longer a credible project. Besides, such debates would be a distraction from the film's unrelenting focus on the terrifying mystery of evil.

The mood of the entire film, which is bleak and oppressive, reflects the genre of film *noir*; nearly all the action occurs in rain and darkness. It is as if the entrance into the city is an entrance into a nihilistic hell. Urban life is so terrifying and enervating that there seems to be nothing worth handing on to the next generation. Devoid of hope for the future, the present seems pointless. Near the middle of the film, Somerset receives a call from Mills's wife asking him to meet her. She reveals to him that she is pregnant and contemplating an abortion because she "hates the city." Somerset confides that he once got a woman pregnant. While she was committed to having the child, he feared bringing the child into the world and gradually "wore her down." Somerset's ambivalence about life reaches its pinnacle in his comment that he knows he "made the right decision" but that every day he "wishes he'd made a different one." Reason and prudence militate against properly human aspirations: the city is inimical to life itself. The quotation from Milton, which the killer leaves at one of the crime scenes, is apt: "Long is the way and hard that out of hell leads up to light."

The ending of the film will tragically vindicate Mills's wife's cynical view of modern urban life. When John Doe unpredictably turns himself in at the police station, the detectives are suspicious, but utterly unprepared for what he has in store for them. The careful viewer is given a hint of what is about to unfold, when just before the killer enters the police station, a clerk yells to Mills that his wife had called. John Doe soon reveals that there are more bodies and offers to take Mills and Somerset to them. As they drive to a remote field, he articulates his vision and denies that his victims are innocent. Only in a society as corrupt as ours would practitioners of vice be called innocent. He complains that we "tolerate" deadly sin. Insisting that John Doe will soon be forgotten, Mills taunts and mocks the killer, who calmly informs Mills that he will be impressed once he sees the complete performance. In the final act, our worst fears are realized, as John Doe has the severed head of Mills's wife delivered to the field. He then provokes Mills into killing him. What are we to make of this depiction of evil?

One possible interpretation of *Seven* is as a modern-day Greek tragedy. Mills's own destruction is at least in part a result of his own everyday evil. It is significant, for example, that Mills's wife could not talk to him about her predicament. In his naïveté and inexperience, he simply would not have understood her hesitancy about bringing life into the living hell that is the modern city. In his imprudent and rash desire to confront evil, he seems to bring the final catastrophe upon himself. His unwillingness to submit his mind to the knowledge of Somerset, his proud taunting of the killer, and his naïve assumption of his own immunity from vice—all these ordinary evils contribute to his demise. Of course, there is no proportion between Mills's vices, which are admittedly mixed with certain virtues, and the punishment that he undergoes. But that disparity is precisely what makes the cultivation of virtue so crucial; in a world awash in depravity, vices, especially those that foster presumption, render us vulnerable. It would undoubtedly have been difficult for anyone in Mills's position at the end of the movie to restrain himself; for Mills it was impossible. Character is destiny. The character to which Mills aspires is that of super-cop; at one point his wife jokingly calls him Serpico. But the contemporary American city is not hospitable to heroes. Because Mills does not yet possess the wisdom that comes from suffering, from years of dreary confrontations with evil, there is a kind of suitability to his downfall. His pride leaves him open to tragedy. He is a classic tragic hero, whose desire for knowledge blinds him to himself. He is so captivated by the killer, by his desire for a fight, that he fails to see his own vices and flaws. He suffers from a debilitating lack of distance and critical reflection. Somerset, who understands the killer better than Mills, has the proper distance, a distance that allows for understanding but avoids the perils of excessive sympathy and self-forgetfulness.

The echoes of classical tragedy and the complex artifice of *Seven* have led some to identify it as neo-*noir*. But *Seven* is even more restrained and emotionally stultifying than film *noir*. *Seven* does not, for instance, admit the possibility of any significant erotic element, represented in film *noir* by an alluring and mysterious woman. There is no *eros* in the marital relationship between Mills and his wife or in the friendship between Somerset and Mills's wife. To say that the film is restrained is not to say that it suggests nothing about how we ought to understand it. The deadly sins provide us with a criterion for understanding the evil of John Doe. The seven capital sins are called deadly not just because they lead to damnation after this life, but because they kill the soul here and now. Vice inflicts its own punishment and issues an invitation to non-being. Of course, human beings are forgetful animals and the further we sink in vice and indifference, the more we are in need of dramatic reminders. The artistic match between the punishment and the sin of the damned is but a way of making more explicit what is already implicit in the way of life they adopted while on earth. This is John Doe's task.

Yet his vocation does not go unquestioned. During their drive outside of the city, amid the taunting of Mills, Somerset interjects the question whether the killer's enjoyment of his act is compatible with martyrdom. Instead of being a martyr for the eradication of evil, he is actually an embodiment of the vices traditionally associated with the devil: envy and pride. His own envy is dramatically realized in his act of killing Mills's wife. By putting Mills in a situation where he will kill him, John Doe admits his own vice and arranges for his own punishment. But he is also proud, even though that sin has been disposed of already. Not only does he take judgment and execution into his own hands, but he lures Mills into sin. John Doe affords himself the gift of non-being that evil inevitably seeks. His punishment is the slightest of all those meted out in the film. But it should have been the most severe, following the principle—articulated in Dante and Milton—that the corruption of the best is the worst.

During one of their discussions, Somerset comments to Mills that the only thing that would meet their expectations of this killer is if he were the devil himself. Somerset quickly adds that he is just human. But it is not clear that Somerset is entirely right. The combination of reflection and creativity with a complete lack of sympathy or clemency makes John Doe something more than merely human. The way he skillfully corners Mills so that Mills has no way out but to become evil is reminiscent of diabolical evil. The ending of the film seems to reverse the initial pattern of establishing an identity between our perspective and that of the killer.

This is mostly because the film develops the characters of Somerset, Mills, and Mills's wife so that we sympathize with them; their misfortune is in some measure our own. They are the only victims we know independently of the killer's appraisal. In spite of the apparent victory of the demonic criminal in *Seven*, the film does not finally create in its audience feelings of sympathy for him. In this way, *Seven* comes closer than Scorsese's *Cape Fear* or *Silence of the Lambs* to making us feel the horror of evil, to inducing in us feelings of anger toward the demonic criminal. But we cannot take refuge in venting our feelings of rage, lest our anger turn to self-destructive vice, as in the case of Mills. Insatiable curiosity, an appraisal of criminals as crazies, and an inordinate desire for knowledge in the form of direct experience of evil—all this is characteristic not just of Mills but of the average viewer of movies like *Seven*. But the average viewer is likely to be so transfixed and numbed by *Seven* that he will fail to reflect upon himself. Thus, he will share Mills's vices.

As always, there is a flip side to the horror induced by demonic wickedness: a subtle admiration for its power and artistry. In his superior artistic control over the entire drama, if not in his purported intentions, John Doe resembles Lecter. The ending underscores the triumph of the artist–serial killer, whose final act overshadows all else. There is little satisfaction of our desire for justice. Only endless torture would be condign punishment for this sort of villain, who is incapable of remorse. In spite of his protestations, his artistry is exhibited not in the renewal of life but in its vivid destruction. John Doe's theology is a heretical version of the medieval view of the role of sermons on the sins. Those sermons presuppose that God's love grants us the freedom to opt for vice instead of virtue and in so doing to reject Him. By reminding us of God's justice, the sermons call us back through his mercy. But John Doe's sermons have no place for freedom or forgiveness; the primary power in *Seven*'s world is not Dante's "love that moves the stars," but a mechanical and malevolent necessity. For all its reliance upon medieval motifs, *Seven* suffers modernity's chief affliction, the silence of God. Since there can be no call to conversion, the Hell of *Seven* is one without prospect of purgatory or paradise. The advantage of *Seven* over its predecessors is that we feel the loss of that larger vision, the absence of what Edmundson calls an affirming myth of *eros* or love.

We are thus left with the signs and symbols of medieval religious pedagogy, but with no avaliable form or way of life in which that pedagogy might make sense. No merciful and provident God speaks through the signs and symbols. In the modern world of *Seven*, God is effectively dead. The loss of that authoritative voice is not a liberation but an enslavement to new forms of tyranny. Without a providence to bring good out of evil, evil endlessly begets evil. Dante's *Inferno* proves an accurate guide to the modern city. The rain, darkness, and filth that saturate the modern city reflect the bog outside the city of Dis in Dante's Hell, where the wrathful, sunk in the mire, struggle to thrash one another.

There is no good life to which one can aspire in this world; the American dream has become an unrelenting nightmare. *Seven* allows for no ironic distance or detached levity. Malevolence is unrelenting and the best we can do is to cultivate certain virtues to fend off disaster. Neither behaviorist psychology nor autonomous creativity offers a way out. The only hope available to us consists in not succumbing to the meaninglessness of it all, but in keeping alive our sense of the injustice and disorder of contemporary life.

Somerset exercises a kind of ancient Greek moderation, a practice of reigning in one's ambitions and expectations that is prudent in a world that is tragic at best. As we noted, there is something transcendent and ennobling about classical tragedy, if only because it educates us about virtue and vice and both presupposes and fosters natural human feelings of pity, fear, and sympathy. By contrast, *Seven* provides no purgation or catharsis: its ending is oppressive and emotionally stultifying. Unlike the exalted nobility of Greek heroes, Somerset is admirable only because he does not give in to apathy, the vice that modern America equates with virtue.

The final note of *Seven* is, however, sober and not entirely negative. After Somerset tells the police chief that he wants to provide whatever Mills needs, he acknowledges that he will "be around," that he is no longer planning to get out. The movie ends with his quoting Hemingway's statement: "The world is a fine place and worth fighting for." He comments, "I agree with the second part." We might restate Somerset's view in this way. Hemingway is wrong about the world: it is not a fine place. The world is wicked; nonetheless, it is worth fighting for. The great temptation? Apathy. And the great task? To exercise a moderation that is not to be confused with apathy, to act out of a chastened passion for justice, a passion that we know in advance will never be satisfied. This brings Somerset dangerously close to being engulfed by nihilism. The key question is why he has not succumbed. He is noble not because of what he achieves, but because of what he can't quite bring himself to do: abandon Mills and the world that has destroyed him. Given all that has transpired, the great mystery is not the existence of evil but the residue of goodness in Somerset, his unquenched thirst for justice.

3

The Banality of Evil

Seven RENEWS THE QUEST FOR EVIL, avails itself of classical motifs from the texts of Dante, Milton, and Shakespeare, and proffers a compelling, if brutal, tragic vision. The film shares the paradoxical aspirations of these classical texts: to render evil in grandly mythic terms and depict it as a kind of death wish, inevitably bringing about its own nothingness. *Seven*'s recourse to the great books is hardly anomalous. These books have informed American reflection on evil since its inception. *Macbeth* was Abraham Lincoln's favorite play. Before Lincoln, Tocqueville observed mothers carrying civilization with them into the wilderness by bringing along the Bible, Milton, and Shakespeare. Yet this entire tradition of thinking about evil has been called into question. The objection is that the penchant for myth necessarily falsifies the phenomenon of evil, bestowing upon it a grandeur and depth that it lacks.

ARENDT'S BANALITY THESIS

The German-born, Jewish philosopher Hannah Arendt crafted the phrase "banality of evil" to describe the phenomenon of Adolf Eichmann, architect of the Nazis' final solution. On her way to Jerusalem to report on Eichmann's trial, Arendt expected to encounter a modern-day Iago or Macbeth, but found neither.[1] What Arendt discovered in Eichmann was a shallowness of motive, a failure to take thought, and more specifically, an inability to adopt the point of view of another. Instead of a complex and mysterious demon, he was simply a law-abiding citizen doing his job, concerned to advance his career. His "normalcy was more terrifying than the atrocities" he committed. In his testimony, Eichmann alternated between claiming that no one can be criticized for doing what he did, that is, for doing his duty and flippantly dismissing the entire affair. He boasted that he would jump in his grave laughing about his orchestration of the final solution. His insouciant manner of relating his crimes was both "horrible and funny."

From her encounter with Eichmann, Arendt developed the apparently novel thesis that evil has "neither depth nor any demonic dimension." Conversely, "only the good has depth and can be radical."[2] Along with her mentor, Karl Jaspers, she focuses on evil's "total banality" and "prosaic triviality" and regards "any hint of myth... with horror." Jaspers goes so far as to say that Shakespeare's "aesthetic sense would lead to a falsification" of evil.[3] Certainly there are dangers, some of which we have discussed, in any aesthetic or dramatic approach to evil. But one wonders whether these risks can be completely avoided. Even Arendt's rather staid retelling of the Eichmann trial involves an artistic reconstruction of some sort. The key question is this: does myth necessarily lead to a glorification of evil, to an exaltation of it, and thus to a covering over of its "prosaic triviality"? As we shall see, this is not the case in Shakespeare's *Macbeth* or in Milton's *Paradise Lost*; nor is it the case in the film *Seven*. These works begin with the apparent grandeur of evil only to reveal its fundamental emptiness.

Arendt's association of evil with banality has been seen as trivializing Eichmann's actions and to some extent exculpating him, since it seems to deprive him of freedom and responsibility. Even if Arendt were right about Eichmann, there are good reasons to resist the universal application of her position. The description of evil as a "mere technique of management," as resulting from a failure to think and a willingness to treat humanity itself as if it were superfluous, is best suited to the sort of evil endemic to modern, bureaucratic regimes. As she notes, banality marks the final stage in the totalitarian annihilation of the world, others, and the self. In spite of these limitations, Arendt's account of evil is highly suggestive. We have already seen that it coincides at least in certain respects with our view of the trajectory of the aesthetics of evil, with its tendency toward a mixture of comedy and horror that renders heroic evil dubious and farcical. As we will soon see, that trajectory can be traced in films like *Natural Born Killers* and *Pulp Fiction*. These films reveal that the banality of evil need not be limited to totalitarian regimes; some version of it may surface in liberal democracies, where the last residues of human greatness have been lost, where life becomes an end in itself. Before we turn to those movies, it will be useful briefly to pursue the relationship between Arendt's banality thesis and the great tradition of reflection on evil.

THE GRANDEUR AND WRETCHEDNESS OF EVIL

Macbeth

Both Shakespeare's Macbeth and Milton's Satan provide instructive comparisons with Eichmann. The characters are not trivial or simple; initially at least, they possess complexity, depth, and grandeur. Nevertheless, both illustrate the way crime is its own punishment. Macbeth fails in his attempt to place himself beyond the human condition and his embrace of nihilism at the end of the play is the logical term of an unyielding pursuit of evil. In that sense, Shakespeare's Macbeth ends up partially confirming Arendt's view that evil lacks depth, that only the good is radical. The same can be said of Milton's Satan, who in spite of his apparent grandeur actually deprives himself of nobility, beauty, and power by pursuing evil, by making evil his good.

When we first meet Macbeth, he has just proved his bravery in battle. On his return, he encounters the weird sisters, the three witches, who inform him of his immanent promotion and predict his future ascent to the throne. Although his prudent comrade, Banquo, warns him that the "instruments of darkness tell us truths;/Win us with honest trifles, to betray's/In deepest consequence" (1.iii.124-126), he is so taken with their promise that he begins to contemplate helping fate along. His ambition soon cools, however, and were it not for his wife's prodding, he likely would have remained content with his subordinate status. When he expresses reservations about their plan, she questions his manhood and accuses him of cowardice. The warrior seems a wimp by comparison with her clarity of purpose and courageous resolve: "I have given suck, and know/How tender 'tis to love the babe that milks me:/I would, while it was smiling in my face,/Have plucked my nipple from his boneless gums/And dashed the brains out, had I so sworn/As you have done to this" (1.vii.54–58). Lady Macbeth invokes supernatural aid to "unsex" her, to free her from feminine compassion. But she badly overestimates the power of masculine resolve; indeed, she is mistaken about the true nature of courage. In terms of self-knowledge, she is her husband's inferior. After the murders, she rapidly deteriorates, entering a trance-like state, haunted by images of blood she cannot wash off her hands. She cannot bear consciousness of her deed.

While Lady Macbeth loses herself rapidly, Macbeth experiences in excruciating and vivid detail his own progress in evil and descent into nothingness. Initially overwhelmed by his murderous deeds and by the impending threat of vengeance, late in the play he is unmoved by shrieks in the night. By the end, he has "supped full with horrors" and "almost forgot the taste of fears." No longer assaulted by visions of the dead, he gains a kind of self-control. But this proves another deception. The more he pursues absolute power, the more he finds himself in the clutches of the evil sisters. When he is told of his wife's death, he utters the oft-quoted words:

> She should have died hereafter;
> There would have been a time for such a word.
> Tomorrow, and tomorrow, and tomorrow
> Creeps in this petty pace from day to day
> To the last syllable of recorded time;
> And all our yesterday's have lighted fools
> The way to dusty death. Out, out, brief candle,
> Life's but a walking shadow, a poor player
> That struts and frets his hour upon the stage

And then is heard no more. It is a tale
Told by an idiot, full of sound and fury
Signifying nothing. (v.v.18–28)

This is one of the most eloquent nihilistic speeches of all time. Macbeth no longer has anything to live for; time itself is empty, void of hope or regret, merely an objective succession of moments. Macbeth experiences the narrative of human life as a cruel and unintelligible anti-providence, a "tale told by an idiot." Nihilism is not, however, the final word of the play; given Macbeth's multiple defeats, we have reason to associate his nihilism, not with the nature of things, but with the consequences of his traitorous and murderous acts. Even though he chooses to fight on and "will not yield," he is hardly possessed of his former grandeur of spirit. The banality of Macbeth at the end is not the almost comic absurdity of Eichmann, who excuses himself by appeal to the fulfillment of a function in society. Instead, it is the despair of a noble soul who suffers the consequences of having embraced evil. *Macbeth* asserts the viability of natural standards of right and wrong, of the subtle, but nonetheless dramatic, links between human society, human nature, and the larger cosmos.

What makes this a peculiar tragedy is that Macbeth is aware from the start that his actions will prove his undoing, that wicked deeds "return to plague the inventor." In the standard Greek tragedy, the hero commits a deed at least partially in ignorance and only later recognizes what he has done and its consequences. Macbeth's recognition comes immediately after the murder, perhaps even in his reflections prior to the deed. He apprehends that nature will counter his revolt with a revolt of its own: "Blood," he notes, "will have blood./Stones have been known to move and trees to speak" (III.iv.122–24). Macbeth's flaw, if we have to pinpoint an outstanding defect in his character, is his lack of true courage. He succumbs to the entreaties of the witches and his wife, not just out of ambition, but out of weakness. And yet he is in many respects a noble character. His eloquence is more than mere rhetorical flourish. He has a fertile imagination and a capacity to perceive his own situation correctly even as he thrusts himself further into misery. Macbeth's grandeur, then, does not result from evil itself but from the residual nobility and excellence of his soul. As he pursues his illusions of omnipotence further, he becomes more impotent and less complex. He thus approaches the simplicity of evil, its inherent nothingness.

The remainder of the play illustrates his descent into a living Hell and the way equivocation and lies destroy not only one's relationships to others but the very meaning of one's life. Having revolted against the codes of nature and civil society, his own nature revolts against him. Soon after the murder, he comments that he has given his "eternal jewel" to the "common enemy of man," the devil, and that death would be preferable to the "restless ecstasy" he now endures. The further he proceeds in his tyrannical task of murdering all potential threats to his power, the more indifferent he becomes to the fate of his own soul, "to return were as tedious as to go over."

The play illustrates something very much like the traditional doctrine of natural law. Nature is so constituted by God that violations of its laws lead inevitably to punishment. The link between the natural and the supernatural, wherein rebellion against order in the state is simultaneously a violation of nature and God, precludes the possibility of envisioning the divine as an arbitrary, omnipotent, and inscrutable being, the dark God of late medieval voluntarism and Descartes's second *Meditation*. Macbeth's punishment is at once willed by God and self-inflicted. His own nature avenges itself on him. In a reversal of Nietzsche's view of nihilism as arising from the attempt to live in accord with an objective and transcendent order of truth and goodness, Macbeth's nihilism is a direct result of his repudiation of such order.

Lest we suppose that the play provides too clean a resolution to the problem of evil, we should recall that the supernatural forces of evil have not been eliminated. They await another soul on which to prey. In such a world, vices leave us vulnerable to assault by preternatural evil powers. Furthermore, although nature rebels against Macbeth, the punishment of nature is insufficient to defeat him and vindicate the good or the innocent. Instead, human beings, especially those with responsibility for the community, must defend themselves against the likes of Macbeth. Finally, there is the possibility that someone more resolute, less complex than Macbeth might actually succeed in attaining and holding power. He fails in part because he remains human, incapable of fully cutting himself off from the nature he shares with other members of his species. Only at the end, when he loses all sense of feeling and conscience, does Macbeth approach Satanic evil. For most of the play, he suffers from a debilitating division between his calculated ambition and his human feelings of sympathy and fear. Hence, the worst evil is not to be found in those who harbor a conflict within them but rather in those whose passions are under the complete control of their reason and who have a clear apprehension of their goal and the means to its attainment.

Paradise Lost

While Iago in *Othello* supplies the chief example of such pure malevolence in Shakespeare's plays, perhaps the most famous and most influential demonic character in the history of Western literature is the Satan of Milton's *Paradise Lost*. The epic is one of the chief sources of the Romantic fascination with the devil, for it sets a dubious precedent of attempting to depict the devil directly. Some readers find Milton's Satan so much more captivating than God, the angels, or Adam and Eve, that they have accused Milton of being of the devil's party. Whatever the flaws in the presentation of the good characters may be, Milton's depiction of Satanic evil is indeed hard to rival, but not perhaps for the reasons usually given.

Milton's Satan has the grandeur and apparent glory of a Homeric hero. Immediately after turning against God and being thrust out of Heaven, he notes his lost glory but counters: "All is not lost; the unconquerable will,/And study of revenge, immortal hate,/And courage never to submit or yield" (1.106-108). He adds, "Though all our glory extinct, and happy state/Here swallowed up in endless misery" yet "mind and spirit remains/Invincible, and vigor soon returns" (1.139-142). In Satan's celebration of his invincible will and courageous rebellion, there is a striking anticipation of the model of demonic heroism that we detected in *The Exorcist*, *Cape Fear*, *Silence of the Lambs*, and *Seven*. In presenting Satan in this way Milton explains why we find evil so alluring and awesome. Moreover, by allowing Satan to voice his own complaint against God, the source of all good, he allows us to recognize that we are often sympathetic to evil. But Milton does not leave it at this. He proceeds to undermine the project of the aesthetization of evil.

Interspersed with the images of Satan's glory and within his words of self-justification are images and words that reveal a much darker and cowardly intent: to prey upon weaker creatures. The satanic goal is to reverse the strategy of providence, which is to bring good out of evil. Attempting to confound the divine plan, the demons devise an anti-providence and plot to bring evil out of good. Their plot itself makes an important concession: goodness is a primordial given; it precedes and makes evil possible. The fundamental division is between the grateful and the ungrateful.

The attentive reader begins to discover in Satan a malicious intent masked by a remarkable capacity for deception, not just deception of others but also deception of self. Milton describes in some detail Satan's self-destruction, the way giving oneself to evil involves a negation of one's being, life, and intellect. On this view, evil is non-being, the absence of an appropriate perfection or goodness. A successful depiction of evil presupposes a rich and supple narration of goodness. Like Shakespeare, Milton captures both the apparent grandeur of evil, its alluring and glittering surface, and its fundamental poverty and emptiness. Evil is nothing.

Just as in *Macbeth*, in *Paradise Lost* supernatural evil remains, awaiting another opportunity to try to bring evil out of good. *Paradise Lost* provides a more explicit anticipation of the final defeat of evil by the supreme power of goodness, but it leaves humanity in a world where its future is uncertain, where each individual risks being defeated by, or conspiring with, evil. The book ends:

The World was all before them, where to choose
Their place of rest, and Providence their guide:
They hand in hand with wandering steps and slow,
Through Eden took their solitarie way. (XII:646-49)

There is no facile transcendence in these works; the only way to overcome the tragedy is go through it, to defeat evil not by avoiding it, but by comprehending it. The strategy in such dramas is to make the "complete" and presently unrealized "pattern" of life so appealing "that it . . . leaves the audience wishing to live their incomplete and as yet potentially tragic lives in the light of the enacted ideal."[4] We live with a tempered hope, not with the self-possessed certainty of success. We aspire to be "lowly wise."

Most artists have not been as daring as Milton in their attempts to depict demonic evil. Instead, they portray merely human evil, the struggle in a noble but imperfect soul between good and evil. The advantage is that human evil can be complex whereas satanic evil is as close to simple evil as is possible. Even Milton gives us a strikingly human devil who deliberates, expresses doubt, and embodies human vices. But Satan's grandeur is residual; it is precisely the depth and complexity of his being, of his original God-given goodness and excellence, that makes his turning to evil so apparently powerful and magnificent. Both Shakespeare and Milton confirm rather than disprove Arendt's thesis that only the good has depth. Revealing its banality, the perverse pursuit of evil as good undermines and negates itself.

By contrast, our contemporary popular culture abounds in simple portrayals of both good and evil. The new problem of evil is fundamentally a problem of goodness, of our artistic failure to find compelling images of virtue and excellence. The most acceptable model of goodness in contemporary Hollywood is the Romantic paragon of the noble savage who embodies a precivilized and childlike innocence. The predictable, Romantic implication is that reasoning, reflection, and adult experience necessarily entail evil. If civilization, with its complex forms of artifice, is the culprit, then Hollywood would seem to be implicated in the very evil it denounces.

THE ROMANTIC REVIVAL
AND THE BANALITY OF GOODNESS

Forrest Gump

The influence of romanticism in contemporary film is perhaps most striking and most instructive in *Forrest Gump*'s celebration of American innocence. *Forrest Gump* reflects in myriad ways the populist films of an earlier Hollywood era. The movie begins with Forrest, a man of quite limited but remarkably functional intelligence, reminiscing about the many pairs of shoes he has worn. Like Woody Allen's Zelig, Gump finds himself present at the most important events of his lifetime, but he is not the chameleon-like character that Zelig is. He plays numerous roles, but his character is unaltered; Forrest remains essentially the same person he was as a child. Others change through their association with Forrest; in fact, any lengthy encounter with him is sure to improve one's attitude and lot in life. After his father left, Gump was raised by his devoted mother, who explains the difficult questions of life with a set of platitudes. Armed with this maternal wisdom, Forrest confronts an array of baffling situations and makes it through the 1960s unscathed.

The film highlights important cultural phenomena from the late 1950s to the 1980s: Elvis, the Civil Rights movement, the Beatles, college football, protests against the Vietnam war, and Apple computer. Every president from Kennedy to Reagan appears in the film. It thus retraces a hotly contested period in American history and invites comparison with the standard liberal genealogy of contemporary America supplied by Oliver Stone. For Stone, the death of Kennedy marks the beginning of the end of the American dream. The escalation of the Vietnam war and the Nixon presidency mark the completion of America's transformation into the evil empire. On Stone's view, we have been in a downward spiral ever since; we now live in an age of absurdity.

Gump concedes that much of American life is absurd, but his levity is gentle, not mocking or cruelly ironic. Forrest is usually bemused by the apparent evil in the world; he frequently misconstrues evil intentions or puts a benign interpretation on what he finds perplexing. For example, during a visit to Washington, D.C., to be decorated as a war hero, he hears the speech of a Vietnam war protester. Forrest's only comment concerns the speaker's repeated use of the "F-word": every time he uses the word, "the people for some reason, well, they cheered."

Forrest is never cynical and always knows what his duty is. He is blessed with his platitudes ("Life is like a box of chocolates," "Stupid is as stupid does," and so forth). He is also blessed with a good will and an oblivion to the offenses and dangers that surround him. Gump embraces all the evils of Stone's America and attempts to restore our faith in the virtues of the simple American. The film thus resurrects the old view of America as a providential fact and contains a kind of civil religion. Forrest's sense of divine providence is of course derived from his mother's, who on her death-bed tells him not to grieve—it is her time. Just do "the best with what God gives you," she counsels him.

That sense of providence is occasionally put into question but never undermined. After Forrest saves his injured superior from the battlefields of Vietnam, Lieutenant Dan, as Forrest affectionately calls him, is not grateful, but angry. Now a cripple with no legs, he berates Gump for cheating him of his destiny, which was to "die with honor" on the field of battle. After Forrest has received the Medal of Honor, traveled the world as a military ping-pong champion, and been on Dick Cavett with John Lennon, he encounters a hostile and desperate Lieutenant Dan, who rages about those who have tried to reconcile him to his fate by pushing Jesus on him. Gump responds, "I'm going to heaven, Lieutenant Dan." Good fortune eventually catches up with Lieutenant Dan when he joins Forrest in a nationally successful shrimp boat enterprise. The pair makes the cover of *Fortune* magazine, Lieutenant Dan thanks Forrest for saving his life, and Forrest comments that Dan has made his "peace with God."

Gump's relationship with Jenny, his childhood sweetheart and the object of his unwavering affection, is sublimated into an American story. Their union reconciles dramatically opposed American narratives. While Forrest is part of the establishment, Jenny embraces the counterculture, where she is repeatedly mistreated by bullying men, becomes a drug addict, and nearly commits suicide. On Forrest's visit Washington, D.C., as a war hero, he meets Jenny and ends up defending her from her peace-loving but abusive boyfriend. As they part, he comments, "I'm glad we were here together in our nation's capital." Later, Jenny returns to Alabama for the July Fourth holiday and during her visit they have sex. Before she leaves, Forrest tells her: "I'm not a smart man but I know what love is." Unbeknownst to Forrest, he has conceived a son. At the end of the film, Jenny calls Forrest to come visit, introduces him to his son, and informs him that she is dying of a mysterious disease. We are thus brought up to the age of AIDS. Given Jenny's immersion in the hippie culture of the 1960s and its sexual revolution, AIDS seems to be rooted in the libertine attitudes of that era. It is clear, however, that little Forrest has turned her life around; she has been converted to Forrest Gump's worldview. After she dies, Forrest Gump, not the counterculture, is left to raise the next generation.

The only point at which Forrest shows deep emotion and confusion is at the end of film, after Jenny has died. As he stands at her grave in the yard of his childhood home, he weeps quietly and wonders whether there really is a destiny shaping events or whether we are "all just floating around accidental, like on a breeze." (The image of a feather being blown gently by a breeze begins and ends the film.) But mere chance does not rule in Gump's world. Showing signs of complexity of both emotion and thought, Gump surmises, "maybe both"—a thesis that suits the very structure of Gump's life, where apparent evils are overcome by unanticipated chance events, events that provide glimpses of a benevolent design in American life. Forrest's return to his childhood home to raise his son suggests that he has never really left home or childhood. In spite of the hint of complexity at the end of the story, Forrest is simple like a child. Indeed, he is even simpler than a child, since children very early on begin to exhibit an incipient complexity that anticipates adult life.

Instead of being an impediment, his disability renders him invulnerable. During the very period when America is losing its innocence, Forrest retains his. Innocence seems to be the path not only to all the important, all-American virtues like diligence, loyalty, honesty, and patriotism, but also to the recovery of the American dream. Vice arises from the capacity for critical reflection, the capacity so prized by those who seek to raise social consciousness. Forrest views evil as an unintelligible occurrence in a world that otherwise makes pretty good sense. At the outset, we are told that Forrest was named for a civil war hero and founder of the Ku Klux Klan. The name is a reminder that "sometimes we do things that, well, just don't make no sense." Forrest never struggles to determine what is right; he never experiences a divided will or even has to fight with himself to bring himself to do what he knows he should. In that sense, his simplicity resembles the mythical life of childhood innocence celebrated in certain strains of Romanticism.

Given that the film pokes fun at the great liberal battles and ideals of the 1960s, it is not surprising that some conservatives applauded the film, while some liberals decried it. Although the film presents Forrest as a sympathetic, even admirable, figure, investing one's ideals in such a simplistic character can be self-subverting. Why not conclude that the only way anyone could continue to believe in an unsullied America is to be as stupid as Forrest?

Gump's simple innocence is hardly a traditional ideal. It is especially not a traditionally religious ideal. Gump is utterly untouched by the effects of Original Sin that, according to Christians, infects every human soul. Moreover, his simplicity serves to minimize evil only by flattening out goodness, by divesting it of any sense of complexity, depth, or greatness. If the contemporary problem of evil is, as I have suggested, largely a problem of our inability to depict goodness in complex, realistic, and attractive ways, then *Gump*'s equation of goodness with Romantic innocence is part of the problem, not the solution.

Natural Born Killers

The Romantic model of goodness surfaces even in the work of Oliver Stone, the most unlikely of places. His *Natural Born Killers* depicts the cross-country murder spree of Mickey and Malory, products of dysfunctional families who achieve fame and national notoriety when the media turn them into cultural icons. In the film's reconstruction of Malory's youth, she stars in a sitcom, complete with a laugh-track, entitled "I Love Malory." The father, played by Rodney Dangerfield, verbally abuses wife and children and has lost all sexual interest in his wife, but finds his daughter irresistible. Mickey, himself abused and scarred indelibly by having witnessed his father's suicide, becomes Malory's liberator. He arrives at the house to deliver a huge sack of bloody red meat and is quickly taken by Malory's comeliness. He soon returns to liberate Malory by killing her parents, and their romantic journey of indiscriminate violence begins.

The "I Love Malory" sequence traces evil not just to the nuclear family, but to our fascination with celebrity. In some of the film's most discordant juxtapositions, Stone alternates between contemporary scenes of violence and scenes of people from the 1950s, sitting comfortably in living rooms watching television. The seeds of the current media celebration of evil were present in that era of apparent American innocence. Americans have such a flimsy sense of self that they derive their identity from television and worship its stars.

Featured on the television show *American Maniacs*, Mickey and Malory become television icons. Their adoring public is mesmerized by footage of their destruction; teenagers think Mickey and Malory are cool. The liberal principles of human dignity recede before the power of celebrity, an amoral force. Of course, the kids concede, "mass murder is wrong . . . we respect human life," but if "we were serial killers, we'd want to be just like" Mickey and Malory. After the duo is captured and goes on trial, fans congregate outside the courthouse, one of them carrying a sign that reads "Kill me, Mickey." To the refrain of "I'm In With the In Crowd," Wayne Gale, host of *American Maniacs*, begins a live, nationally-broadcast interview with Mickey. When Gayle informs him that the only murderer to have received higher ratings was Manson, a resigned Mickey admits, "It's pretty hard to beat the king."

The broadcast provokes a riot in the jail and affords Mickey an opportunity to escape. Accompanied by Gayle and his camera, he begins wiping out the prison staff. Gayle eventually joins in, kills a policeman, and gushes about his new found sense of liberation. Mickey and Mallory are reunited, and in an act that concisely expresses the simplistic morality of the film, kill Gayle, saying he was just part of the problem.

The film is most successful in its stylistic elements. It employs unusual and disorienting camera angles, alternates between color and black and white, and uses a remarkable variety of musical genres, from the predictable hard rock to country, ballads, love songs, and even opera. (Operatic music accompanies a slow motion shot of a knife, hurled by Mickey at one of his first victims, flies through a plate glass window and into the body of the victim.) The overt and ample use of the aesthetics of evil puts the audience at a certain distance from the murder and mayhem of the film. As critics have noted, Stone lets the viewer know he is making a comedy, but what sort of comedy remains unclear. *Natural Born Killers* is not a comedy that indulges in light comic-book violence; instead, the graphic violence sickens, stupefies, and desensitizes. In his introductory comments to the video release of *Natural Born Killers*, Stone provides a kind of sermon on the 1990s as an "age of absurdity." The appropriate tone is "black humor." But the humor is not graveyard or prison humor that supplies momentary comic relief or seeks to transcend absurdity through absurdity.

In fact, the film is torn between moralism and the pure comedy of evil; in the end, Stone cannot decide whether he is a preacher or a comedian. In spite of his remarks about comedy, Stone wants to achieve clarity about the nature of evil in our time, especially about its intimate connection with the media. In this, Stone reiterates the neoconservative criticism of Hollywood and the media for cultivating villains by raising them to the status of celebrities. The problem with Stone's approach is that it is a dead end. There is nothing independent of Hollywood, since it has already reconfigured society in its own image. This is the Romantic corollary to *Gump*'s pristine innocence: wherever civilization and artifice dominate, we lose our natural goodness and become evil. In *Killers*, no one is human; all are media inventions. In his interview with Gayle, Mickey claims we have all done something that merits serious punishment—no one is innocent.

The only alternative is a complete rejection of civilized, American life. In the desert, Mickey and Malory encounter an elderly Indian and his grandson who offer them food and shelter. The young Indian asks his grandfather what malady afflicts the visitors. The grandfather states that they have become demons from too much television. During the night, Mickey awakens from a recurring nightmare of childhood beatings to attack and kill the Indian. Malory rails against him: "Bad, Bad, Bad." Noting that the Indian took them in and fed them, she exclaims, "You killed life." The only character in the film whose death is undeserved, the Indian is the exception that proves the rule about American civilization. His innocence resides not in what he has but in what he lacks: familiarity with the dominant American way of life. There is more than a residue here of the Romantic ideal of goodness as embodied in the precivilized noble savage about whom Rousseau asserts that his ignorance of vice is more profitable than our knowledge of virtue.

One of the problems with the film's attempt to provide a moral or message concerns the significance of its title. The story traces their violence to the dysfunctional family and the media. If that is so, just how "naturally born" are their homicidal tendencies? One is inclined to be suspicious of any causal account of evil in a movie that is intentionally beyond any sense of proportion. The ending of the film with footage from contemporary media—of O. J., Rodney King, and Waco—recalls Stone's introductory comments connecting the film to the current decade of absurdity and underscores the media's fascination with evil and its creation of cult heroes out of murderers. But it does not get us any closer to what evil is, except perhaps to point us in the direction of the media itself. By conflating different kinds of

evil—that of the jealous, controlling husband, institutional-
ized racial prejudice, and the government's arrogant bureaucratic blunders—the final footage flouts the task of making
distinctions about evil.

Perhaps few viewers and film critics would juxtapose
Gump and *Killers*. Both purport to be comedies, but only
Gump has a classical comic structure, suggesting a benevolent design behind American life. *Killers* bestows the palm
of victory upon demonic forces; in this America, everyone is
either possessed or wants to be possessed. *Gump*'s simplicity spurns the complexity and freedom of adult life, while
Killers seems to present evil as complex, alluring, and liberating. But where everyone is equally and fundamentally
implicated in evil, there can be no freedom or responsibility.
As different as they appear, *Gump* and *Killers* share certain
Romantic assumptions about goodness and evil; the two films
are mirror images of one another. The banality of goodness
meets the banality of evil; neither offers anything more than
a crude and literal metaphysics. Not surprisingly, both films
spoof the classical theme of the quest. At one point, Gump,
known from his youth for his running ability, runs from one
side of the country to the other. He becomes a celebrity;
everyone wonders what his cause is and groupies begin to
follow him hoping he will divulge the wisdom behind his
journey. But they are disappointed. Just as Forrest began
running with no goal in mind, so he stops for no apparent
reason. Mickey and Malory also cover a good deal of
America on their killing spree, and Stone invites us to come
along on his quest for evil. Again, the quest is not so much
thwarted as mocked, sublimated into entertainment. We
have a choice between equally unintelligible routes: random
acts of kindness or arbitrary acts of destruction.

THE RECONSTRUCTION OF SOCIETY

One way out of the Romantic trap of *Gump* and *Killers* is to present innocence itself as at least inchoately complex and to explore the possibility of a tragic outcome to the encounter between innocence and the less than innocent world. This is the successful strategy of *Sling Blade* (1996). Although it shares with Romanticism an absence of adult models of goodness, it depicts the main character, Karl Thornton, a retarded adult, as complex. The movie opens with his release from a psychiatric hospital, where he has been held since committing a childhood murder with a sling blade. The film follows his reintroduction to society, and builds toward an inevitable, violent climax, in which he repeats his previous act of murder. He is neither blithely invulnerable to evil nor detached from the suffering of others; he is even a fairly astute observer and judge of character. His acts of violence are always a response to real evil; given his limited social skills and his inability to ignore the affliction of others, he has no other option. Thus do circumstances and character conspire to bring about a tragic ending.

Romanticism is, as we have noted, a complex phenomenon and some of the complexity is reflected in our popular culture. For many, Romanticism provides a path out of the chains of civilization back to a liberating nature, however construed. But the temptation, especially when Romanticism fuses with a certain conception of Enlightenment progress, is to reform society in light of the Romantic vision. This was Rousseau's great project: to reconstruct society, to reconcile instinct and reason, the individual and the community, freedom and obedience to law. Given the antithesis between nature and society with which Rousseau begins, the project seems quixotic, likely to give birth to a progressive vision of society in the form of an endless revolution. In Hollywood, the tension between instinct, passion, spontaneity, and creativity, on the one hand, and repressive, bourgeois institutions, on the other, is a source of tragic drama. The conflict is rather successfully portrayed in the film *Dead Poets Society*, with Robin Williams as the inspiring poetry teacher who fosters in his students a desire for authenticity that puts them at odds with the authoritarian world of administrators and parents. When a gifted student angers his father, an emotionally distant and iron-willed man, by violating his prohibition against acting in the school play, the boy's frustration and despair lead him to commit suicide. Because the boy's plight is depicted in such noble terms, some blamed the film for glorifying suicide. From the perspective of our study, the deeper import of the film is this: it illustrates the way the conflict between civilization and the Romantic authenticity of self-expression can foster the longing to transcend the societal code of good and evil. We are, admittedly, not yet at a nihilistic stage, since *Dead Poets Society* does appraise ways of life as noble or base, ranking them in terms of their authenticity. The question, as we have seen with Nietzsche, is whether the notion of authenticity or of artistic self-creation inevitably leads to nihilism.

Titanic

These Romantic themes are equally, if much less obviously, operative in the big Oscar winner of 1997, the epic *Titanic*. The story, which can be called "romantic" in the sense in which that term is now ordinarily used, pits the lower-class, but spontaneous and artistically gifted, Jack Dawson, played by Leonardo DiCaprio, against old world money, with its shallow formality and petty sense of superiority. On board the great ship, Dawson meets and then vies for the affection of the affluent Rose, whose disaffection from the members of her class, including her family and her fiancé, grow as she becomes romantically involved with Dawson. Their star-crossed love, fostered by their shared taste for art and free self-expression, competes with the ship *Titanic* as the central spectacle of the film. One wonders to what extent the makers of the film were conscious of the multiple significance of the ship itself. By underscoring the engineer's optimism and the crew's naïve and negligent trust in his proclamations that the *Titanic* is unsinkable, the film displays the tragic hubris of modern technology and Enlightenment progress. But the ship symbolizes more than the Enlightenment project of mastering nature. It is also a Romantic symbol, an artifact of great beauty, deservedly inspiring awe. The sense of omnipotence the ship conveys to those on board is evident in the famous scene where Jack climbs to the head of the bow of the ship, extends his arms, and exclaims, "I'm the king of the world!" *Titanic* allows us to see something about Romanticism that the apparently heroic love between Jack and Rose conceals. In the figure of the ship itself, two forms of modern hubris, that of Enlightenment science and of Romantic rebellion, converge. Both are excessive, inordinately indulging one or another feature of human life to the exclusion of other features and other persons. The love between Jack and Rose attracts us because they are so attractive and because those they oppose are so obviously cold and callous. But it is hard to see their love as much more than adolescent and self-absorbed. In the climactic scenes, Jack and Rose do exhibit more fellow feeling toward their doomed shipmates than do the members of the privileged class, but they can be deemed virtuous only by contrast to the vices of others. Once again, Romanticism fails to produce a mature and complex vision of goodness.

What makes *Titanic* a romance in the popular meaning of the term is its focus on a love that isolates the lovers and elevates them above others. One possible development of this motif is the unleashing of limitless desire, which, as Sade suggested, is especially aroused when it confronts prohibitions. This motif finds its most dramatic expression in adulterous liaisons. But what happens when society eases its prohibitions, when something like adultery is no longer an act of rebellion but rather a common practice? Might we then discover the "dull monotony of passion," that adultery could be as routine and enervating as marriage?

The Ice Storm

A recent film by Ang Lee, *The Ice Storm*, illustrates precisely these lessons about sexual desire and adultery. The film focuses on two families in the posh suburb of New Canaan, Connecticut, in November 1973. The film captures affluent, suburban family life in the wake of the sexual revolution. The characters in *The Ice Storm* lack passion and self-knowledge; their despair is so deep they fail to recognize it. It is essentially the story of two families, with the father of one and the mother of the other engaged in an affair. After one of their mid-afternoon adulterous liaisons, Ben lies next to

Jamie and rambles on about personal problems. Obviously put off, Jamie curtly states, "You're boring me. . . . I have a husband." Ben, played by Kevin Kline, is married to Elena, with whom he has two teenage children, Paul and Wendy. Jamie, played by Sigourney Weaver, is married to Jim, with whom she has two sons, Mikey and Sandy. The two families socialize regularly and live within walking distance of one another. Although they are oblivious to it, they lead terrifyingly ordinary lives, devoid of communication, love, longing, or hope. Despite their wealth, or perhaps because of it, Elena and Wendy, mother and daughter, both shoplift. The brothers, Mikey and Sandy, are socially awkward; the younger one, Sandy, is an introverted pyromaniac, launching explosives from the family's deck. When their father returns home from a business trip to Houston and exclaims, "Hey guys, I'm back," Mikey nonchalantly asks, "You were gone?"

Little actually happens in the film, but its very stillness brings home the emptiness of the lives led by the characters. *The Ice Storm* depicts the living death of its characters in an unadorned style. While the film immerses the audience in a nihilistic world, it provides us with an awareness, a perspective that the denizens of that world lack. We are led to see and feel the horror of this way of life. But the mechanism by which we achieve a certain distance from the world of the characters is not that of comic detachment or ironic freedom. The principal artistic device is that of natural sounds and images. To produce its benumbing and instructive effects, *The Ice Storm* makes manifold use of ice.

On the crucial evening in *The Ice Storm*, Paul is at a party in New York City, both sets of parents attend a "key party" where the wives' selection of keys from a bowl determines who will escort them home, Wendy visits Sandy, and Mikey wanders through the frozen woods and streets. As the events of the evening unfold, the ice envelops and covers everything—roads, trees, windows, and walking paths. The evening will witness Ben's drunken and embarrassingly public attempt to retain Jamie as his lover, Elena and Jim's artless act of car-seat copulation (a feeble attempt to revenge themselves on their unfaithful spouses), Wendy's seduction of the disturbed and barely pubescent Sandy, and finally, Mikey's death by electrocution from a downed power line. When Ben finds Mikey sprawled out on the side of the road, he takes his body home where Elena and Jim have just arrived, where his former lover Jamie is already in bed, and where his daughter, Wendy, and Sandy have just emerged from bed. With the exception of Paul, the two families are now reunited in the face of an actual death. Still incapable of comprehending their situation or of expressing profound feeling, they exchange looks of fear and grief, even some tears and hugs, but few, if any, words.

Only Paul, the son of Elena and Ben, who attends a boarding school in the city, shows any sign of transcending the world of New Canaan. Although he is not presented as a remarkably deep or unusual teenager, he has a healthy crush on a classmate, played by Katie Holmes (whom he refuses to molest when she collapses in his arms at a party). He also reads Dostoevsky and comic book stories about the Fantastic Four, whose predicament frames the entire story. The film opens and ends with Paul returning on a commuter train from his evening in New York. The first memorable sounds we hear are of the train crackling along the icy track. As he sits silently reading, a voice-over, identifiably the voice of Paul himself, describes a typical challenge faced by the Fantastic Four, when a nihilist turns the son of one of the heroes into a live atom bomb. What makes these superheroes different is that they are all family and that means that "the more power you have, the more you have the capacity to do damage without knowing it." After we have seen that lesson amply and numbingly illustrated during the film, we return to Paul and the Fantastic Four at the end. Paul's voice explains the role of the "negative zone" in the comic series. It is an inversion of our expectations, where "things don't work out," and which "tempts us to go all the way in."

The restrained aesthetic of *The Ice Storm* captures the paralysis of life in the "negative zone," the subtle, cumulative, perhaps largely unintentional destruction wrought by ordinary acts of evil. The paradox is that, while the characters are isolated from one another, trapped in themselves, their lives are inextricably bound up with one another. Individualism depletes rather than enriches the self. The pursuit of pleasure is self-defeating; instead of liberating passion, we are left with merely mechanical acts of sexual congress. Thus does the banality of evil find its finest contemporary expression.

RECOVERING THE COMIC QUEST: *Pulp Fiction*

In the gap between the unknowing and unfeeling point of view of its characters and that of the artist and audience, *The Ice Storm* avoids implicating its own artistry in what it exhibits. Without a divergence of perspective, it seems that the artist, however much he might protest the contrary, must be complicit in what he depicts. Such has often been the judgment of one of the most celebrated films of the last decade, Quentin Tarantino's *Pulp Fiction*. On the surface, this film moves us a step closer to the normalization of evil and comic-book violence. Like *Killers*, it glamorizes gangster life and derives much of its humor from the casual, conventional depiction of that way of life. Roger Shattuck insists that the normalization of evil in *Pulp Fiction* "neutralizes it—absorbs it into ordinary life, broken by a few thrills and laughs, and desensitizes us to evil."[5] Shattuck rightly rejects the argument that the film mocks the "industry's crass exploitation of violence"; rather, it is "complicit with the violence it depicts." But Shattuck overlooks a novel feature of the film: the suggestion that someone seemingly at home in its world may awaken to the possibility of an entirely different way of life, to discover the possibility of an integrating and ennobling purpose, and thus embark upon a quest, this time not for evil, but for goodness.

Pulp Fiction consists of a series of interrelated short stories, of which the principal concerns a gangster duo, Vincent, played by John Travolta, and Jules, played by Samuel L. Jackson. Although a number of pivotal events occur in the series of overlapping narratives, what happens is no more important than what the characters say about what happens. The primacy of dialogue is evident in a number of scenes. In the opening, a husband and wife team of robbers decide to rob the restaurant where they are eating, but only after they discuss the drawbacks of stealing from banks and liquor stores. The last option is beginning to present serious communication problems because of the predominance of foreign liquor store owners. As the husband enumerates the risks involved in hitting the usual places, the wife becomes incredulous and asks: "What then, day jobs?" He suggests:

"Nobody ever robs restaurants—why not?" A subsequent scene shows Vincent and Jules, on the way to a hit, discussing the differences between McDonald's restaurants in Amsterdam and the United States and chuckling over the foreign name of the "Quarter-pounder with Cheese," the "Royale with Cheese." But their most humorous exchange occurs in the same restaurant where we have just left the married robbers. Jules is explaining that he will not eat pork because the pig is a "filthy animal." Vincent presses him and asks about dogs:

> **Vincent:** How about dogs? Dogs eat their own feces.
> **Jules:** I don't eat dog, either.
> **Vincent:** Yes, but do you consider a dog a filthy animal?
> **Jules:** I wouldn't go so far as to call a dog filthy, but they're definitely dirty. But a dog's got personality. And personality goes a long way.
> **Vincent:** So by that rationale, if a pig had a better personality, he'd cease to be a filthy animal?
> **Jules:** We'd have to be talking about one charmin' m————n' pig. I mean he'd have to be ten times more charmin' than that Arnold on *Green Acres*.

The allusion to the television pig Arnold is perhaps the most humorous example of an inevitable feature of the dialogue: commentary on popular culture. Nowhere is this commentary more pronounced than in the scene where Vincent escorts Mia, his mob boss's wife, to dinner at a 1950s style diner, where Marylin Monroe is a waitress and Buddy Holly, a busboy. When Vincent effortlessly identifies the various Hollywood personalities working at the diner, Mia is impressed and comments, "Pretty smart." Then, in an obvious spoof of Travolta's *Saturday Night Fever* routine, Vincent and Mia enter a dance contest. What is the significance of all these references to pop culture?

In the absence of the old distinction between high and low art, sophistication now involves witty commentary on pop culture. Art has narcissistically turned in upon itself as if there were no reality independent of it. Or better—art reflects life but life itself is now indistinguishable from pop culture. The nihilism underlying such a world suits the tone of a moderately dark comedy like *Pulp Fiction*.

Pulp Fiction normalizes the world of drugs and crime and treats it comically. Vincent's dealer promotes heroin by proclaiming, "It's making a comeback." When Vincent questions the quality of the heroin and reminds the dealer that he's been in Amsterdam, the dealer counters, "I'll take the Pepsi challenge with that Amsterdam s—t anytime." After they have concluded their transaction, as if to underscore the Ozzie and Harriett normalcy of the life of drugs, the dealer calls to his wife from the bedroom: "Honey, will you get me some baggies from the kitchen?" None of the characters in *Pulp Fiction* adopts an ironic, mocking tone toward drug-free, civilized life because the life of gangsters and drug users is itself conventional.

The film follows through on the conventionality of evil more fully and more persuasively than does *Natural Born Killers*. On this score, it is interesting to note that Tarantino wrote the original script for *Killers* but, after disagreements with Stone, his name was removed from the credits. A crucial point of contention was Tarantino's penchant for leaving "things unexplained." The need to present an explanation makes Stone's *Killers* a thoroughly ambivalent, if not self-refuting, film. Stone cannot let go of the pretense of moral critique. The pointlessness of life seems to be reflected in the nonlinear structure of the film, in the impossibility of narrative unity. This, however, is but one possible interpretation of the absence of narrative unity. Leaving "things unexplained" does indeed undermine the sort of closure that characterizes most of the films we have examined thus far. Those narratives are infused with a relentless and unyielding malevolent force, a force that eliminates freedom and terrorizes our imagination by subjecting it to the aesthetics of evil. Given the sort of deterministic unity operative in contemporary treatments of evil, *Pulp Fiction*'s openendedness may be to its advantage. The film does not in fact leave us with mere chance, though stories intersect and coincidences occur. What we are to make of these intersections and coincidences is the central question of the film.

The issue is brought out most clearly in a sequence in which, during a hit, a gunman surprises Vincent and Jules, aims directly at them from a short distance, shoots, and misses. Jules is astounded, "We should be f——g dead. . . . This is divine intervention . . . a miracle." Vincent dismissively responds, "This s—t happens." In the subsequent scene, they are driving in a car, when Vincent's gun goes off and kills a backseat passenger. Vincent excuses himself by stating that it was an "accident . . . the gun went off . . . I don't know why." The coupling of these two chance events, one benevolent, the other destructive, complicates Jules's claim that he "felt the hand of God." What, finally, are we to make of the appeal to the miraculous?

What we know is that the belief in divine intervention immediately puts Jules at odds with the "cool" world of evil that his partner, Vincent, still inhabits. When Jules announces that he is giving up crime to embark on a religious quest, Vincent accuses him of "deciding to be a bum." Vincent, the gangster, adopts without any hint of irony the posture of conventional society and defends its commitment to the Puritan work ethic. When this conversation occurs, we already know, because of Tarantino's reversing of temporal sequences, that Vincent will die in a chance encounter in which he is shot with his own gun. Is his bad luck a divine judgment on his lack of faith, a fitting punishment for his failure to discern the work of the hand of God? Or is it all mere chance? The movie never resolves the issue; indeed, such a resolution is impossible in a world with no ultimate structure or unity, in which chance events point simultaneously in multiple and contradictory directions. But this need not be construed as evidence of failure. *Pulp Fiction*'s world of signs and wonders intelligently raises the crucial questions and prudently refuses to answer them. Shattuck's judgment that *Pulp Fiction* does not see "around or beyond the horrible actions that it portrays with the utmost cool" is only partially correct. Such a serious investigation would take us out of the world the characters presently inhabit. Jules continues to insist that he is going to do just that, retire from gangster life and wander the earth like Cain in *Kung Fu*. Here we must also recall the biblical Cain and the first fratricide. God intervened both to accuse Cain and to mark him with a sign to keep him from being killed.

Both in its vignette structure and in its explicit reference to its fictional or constructed character, *Pulp Fiction* raises fundamental questions about art and the possible unity of a narrative. On the one hand, its willingness to entertain the possibility of the miraculous points in the direction of a way out of, or at least a way through, the semiotic Hell in which we find ourselves. It raises the crucial question of classical comedies: the role of chance or coincidence in opening up the possibility of a higher and more comprehensive perspective. It also implicitly raises the question of who is orchestrating events and to what end. Jules and Vincent differ over how to interpret their remarkable good fortune. Although we do not know what the ultimate result of believing in a miracle would be, the belief has already begun to transform Jules, who is seriously considering an entirely different way of life. The "miraculous" saving of their lives cuts off an otherwise unending chain of violence. Jules's interpretation of the "miracle" frees him from the deterministic gangster world. One sign that he has already begun to live that life is his change of mind about a passage from the prophet Ezekiel, a passage about the wrath of God that he quotes to his victims before killing them. He no longer interprets that passage or sees his own life in terms of divine vengeance. Moreover, he defuses potential violence in the hold-up attempt in the coffee shop. Perhaps nothing more can be pursued in this story, since the quest that Jules is contemplating would take him out of the cyclical, redundant world he inhabits; it would set him on a new and more arduous path. So, divine intervention is an undeveloped, but pregnant, suggestion. Unless we follow Jules, we are left with no code to decipher the multiple signs and symbols of contemporary life. Without that code, we might be tempted to adopt a thoroughly comic and ironic take on our nihilistic condition.

The character of Jules suggests the possibility of reviving the premodern, especially scriptural, conception of man as a wanderer on the earth; the New Testament reminds us that "we have here no lasting city." The Enlightenment project of creating a utopian city, where human needs are transparently detected and readily satisfied, spurns such counsel. As we noted in the last chapter, in such a context the apparently irrational quest for evil can be a sign of health or life. If *Seven* fends off nihilism by recovering the tragic aspiration for justice in the modern world, *Pulp Fiction* suggests a way through that world by reviving the potentially comic quest. In Jules, we see the shift from God as vengeful to God as providential guide in a world where all are in need of mercy, the world we enter at the end of Milton's *Paradise Lost.* This allows for a new twist on Mickey's assertion in *Natural Born Killers* that everyone is guilty and deserving of punishment. It hints at the possibility of transcending the malevolent determinism that pervades so many contemporary films.

4

Normal Nihilism

WE BEGAN with the great nineteenth- and twentieth-century analysts of nihilism: Tocqueville, Nietzsche, and Arendt. They describe it as a state where everything is permitted, where there is no scale of higher and lower, noble and base. All three detect links, both obvious and subtle, between certain types of democratic liberalism and nihilism. To see the artistic and cultural consequences of nihilism, we focused on the topic of evil, on its aesthetics, its banality, and its link to the comedic. We have seen anticipations of the comic turn in the treatment of nihilism in films like *Cape Fear* and *Silence of the Lambs*. We have also considered two more explicitly comic, if quite different, approaches to evil in a nihilistic world in *Natural Born Killers* and *Pulp Fiction*.

The latter films break down the opposition between conventional society and the rebellious criminal. If Stone's film is a rather uneasy mixture of serious moralism and comic nihilism, Tarantino's movie is both a more relaxed and a more serious comedy. The casual ordinariness of criminal life strikes a relaxed comic tone; evil has "neither depth nor any demonic dimension." So it seems that there is no great mystery to be pondered; the search for evil is over. And yet, after having been inexplicably saved from certain death, Jules promises to begin a quite different sort of quest, a quest for goodness under the tentative signs of divine providence. Thus it points toward the possibility of a comic ending, wherein characters are brought to a more elevated state, a state that surpasses their merits and expectations.

If there is no possibility of either the classically tragic or the classically comic take on nihilism and evil, then the next most likely stage is that of normal nihilism. Nihilism is no longer wrestled with, heroically embraced, or subsumed within some larger narrative. Instead, it becomes an unspoken assumption. What is peculiar about the late twentieth century is the way meaninglessness has indeed become both a prevailing, if unremarked, supposition and a fertile source of comedy. Although it has competitors like *The Simpsons*, no cinematic or television production has tapped into this surprisingly rich comic source as fully or entertainingly as has *Seinfeld*. As we learn in one episode, *Seinfeld* is a show about "absolutely nothing." Of course, it is not all that novel for the plots of sitcoms to focus on the seemingly insignificant events of daily life. What is quite novel and remarkably creative is the depth and complexity of *Seinfeld*'s insight into the comical consequences of life in a world devoid of any ultimate meaning or fundamental purpose. This is the basis of *Seinfeld*'s comic nihilism.

Seinfeld is important not just because it suits our genealogy of evil in a nihilistic culture. As Michael Medved has noted, popular culture in contemporary America—that is,

Hollywood culture—is mediated more through television than through film. If we are right to see in *Seinfeld* a form of comic nihilism, then its presence on prime time television is quite telling. *Seinfeld*'s remarkably successful television run is roughly coextensive with the 1990s and it captures the absurdity of the decade better than Stone's *Natural Born Killers*, because it does not share the latter's shallow moralism. *Seinfeld*'s thoroughly comic take on nihilism converges with developments in recent films.

DARE TO SAY YES: *Trainspotting*

By way of a prelude to an extended examination of *Seinfeld*, we will consider a surprisingly similar approach to evil and nihilism in the film *Trainspotting*, which succeeds precisely where *Killers* fails. The film, set in Scotland with indigenous actors, does not immediately reflect American culture in the way *Killers* sets out to. But it does play off of a highly influential American vision of the good life, a vision that has been exported to every corner of the globe. At the beginning of the movie, the main character, Renton, speaks in praise of drug use as a way of life. He cleverly and derisively turns on its head every parent's, schoolteacher's, and politician's slogan about a drug-free America. Admitting that you could "choose your future . . . you could choose life," he counters, "why would I choose to do a thing like that." Playing upon our nearly bankrupt language of choice, he mocks, "I chose not to choose life." Posing to himself the next likely question, about the reasons for his choice, he responds that "there are no reasons. Who needs reasons when you've got heroin?" The outside world thinks heroin is all about "misery, despair, and death and all that s—t, but what they forget is the pleasure of it." As Renton sees it, the law-abiding world of drug-free society is itself all about pleasure; it just pursues its petty pleasures by more complicated means and in less satisfying ways. An ordinary life of conformity is caught up in all sorts of distracting worries about things like paying bills and making human relationships work. But a "true and sincere drug habit" clarifies things. It gives simplicity and unity to one's life: the only worry is about scoring. Given conventional society's fixation on sexual pleasure, Renton's claim on behalf of heroin is impressive: if you take the best orgasm you have ever had and multiply its pleasure by a thousand, you still have not reached the experience of heroin. By contrast, conventional pleasure is tepid and always adulterated by consciousness of past regrets and future duties or projects.

Like *Killers*, the film indulges in the aesthetics of evil and black comedy. The film alternates so often and so quickly between horror and comedy that it becomes hard to separate them. Most of the scenes in which we approach the horror of drug addiction have a decidedly comic edge to them. In one disgusting scene, Renton takes a drug in the form of a suppository and in his desperate need to relieve his bowels forgets about the pill. We are then treated to fantastic images of him diving head first into a toilet, billed as the filthiest in Scotland, and swimming through a sort of reservoir. Pill in hand, he emerges triumphantly from the toilet. Near the end of the movie, he attends a funeral for a friend and learns that the fellow was so high he failed to clean up after his cat, contracted a disease from ingesting cat feces, and died. The cat? He's fine.

Only one scene in the film captures the numbing terror of drug life. In the home where most of the drug use occurs, a child of one of the addicts crawls aimlessly and unobtrusively from room to room. When the party is interrupted by the piercing screams of the mother as she discovers the child's dead and discolored face, Renton observes with foreboding that this time things will not get better. But as the mother's wailing subsides, she requests a hit, which Renton supplies but only after giving himself one. The image of the dead child lasts but a moment, and the matter is never mentioned again. Renton is wrong: things do get better, or at least return to their typical state. In the repetitive, circular world of drugs, there is no novelty, no possibility of progress or regress, no ultimate hope or despair.

The film continues the reversal of the relationship between evil and law-abiding society that we have already noted in other films, although there is not as sharp a contrast between the two as there was in *Cape Fear* or *Silence*. Renton is only moderately interested in offending, and not at all inclined to terrorize, civil society. He meets society more on its own terms: the pursuit of pleasure. Like the rest of us, he wants to be left alone to live his life as he sees fit. The "principle drawback" to a life of addiction is putting up with the endless moralizing from straight friends and family members, who berate Renton about polluting his body and wasting his life. As his subversive deployment of our democratic language of choice and consent indicates, we are already beyond good and evil. Mocking the language of Enlightenment rationality, he describes the decision of his group to go back on drugs as a fully informed, democratic choice. Autonomy gives way to aesthetic self-creation.

The evil of Renton distinguishes itself from the morality of conventional society by its forthright honesty and its blatant exercise of a will to pleasure. Conventional society is banal by contrast. Yet the evil of Renton is itself banal by comparison with that of the invading spirit in *The Exorcist,* Hannibal Lecter in *Silence of the Lambs,* or John Doe in *Seven.* There is nothing superhuman or especially diabolical about Renton. His alternation between the terrifying and the absurd is somewhat reminiscent of Arendt's depiction of Eichmann. If Eichmann turns our language of duty against our basic intuitions about human dignity, Renton performs the same reversal with our language of free choice and informed consent. In other respects, however, Renton's banality is quite different from that of Eichmann, whose banality is the result of his unflagging conformity to the dictates of conventional society. Renton is no totalitarian, though he does indiscriminately treat everyone as an instrument for the maximization of his own pleasure. He is, moreover, never unintentionally or unconsciously funny in the way Eichmann was. Renton's sense of irony, a source of much of the film's dark humor, evinces at least a certain level of psychic complexity, whereas Eichmann was all surface. What little depth Renton may possess is a result of his dynamic affirmation of the eternal recurrence of drug life and the utter poverty of the purported goodness of drug-free society.

In the film's final segments, Renton and his buddies plan and successfully pull off a deal to buy drugs cheap and sell them for profit. After Renton takes off with all the money, he admits (to us) that he has no good reason for taking the money except that most of the guys would have done the same thing to him if given the opportunity. The film ends with a monologue: "The truth is I'm bad but I'm going to change. . . . I'm going straight and choosing life. . . . I'm going to be just like you: the job, the family, the f——g big television, the washing machine, the car, good health, low cholesterol, dental insurance, mortgage . . . looking ahead, the day you die." His knowing and inviting smile as he looks directly at us in the final scene implies that we get the joke, that he is already one of us or, more pointedly, that we are already one with him. If we admire his resolve and his clarity, then we are tempted to share his view of the essential sameness of drug and straight culture, or rather of the inferiority of straight to drug culture. Renton's affirmation of the cyclical character of drug life is opposed to the linear structure of Enlightenment progress, whose chief contemporary embodiment is the life of endless accumulation coupled with the futile and degrading attempt to fend off death.

Once again, conventional society is indicted for its hypocrisy and cowardice. Insofar as we agree with the indictment and adopt Renton's posture of ironic distance from society, we prove ourselves at least momentarily as daring as he. The problem for most of us is that we will return to our lives of paying bills and lowering our cholesterol. If we can find no higher goals than those of endless accumulation, and if our heroism peaks at daring to say no to drugs, our life looks pointless and comically hollow. One of Arendt's ways of describing nihilism is as a state where life is an end itself, where nothing higher than the mere continuation of existence assumes public significance.

In its detached, ironic take on nihilism, in its accentuation of pleasure over terror, and in its concentration on the cyclical character of a nihilistic world, *Trainspotting* confirms many of our theses about evil and nihilism. First, although the film is obviously a satire of capitalist-consumer culture, its indictment cuts deeper, mocking the very foundations of liberal modernity. It puts in question our moderate and thoroughly conventional understanding and practice of ideals like freedom of choice, equality, and consent. The film is a dramatic illustration of the thesis of Nietzsche and Tocqueville that certain forms of democratic liberalism naturally generate nihilism. Second, the advent of nihilism brings not chaos and shapelessness but a mechanical and deterministic narrative structure, a structure that reflects the shrinking of human aspiration and the constraining of human freedom. Third, the ultimate trajectory of the narrative approach to nihilism is in the direction of comic irony and the petty laughter of Nietzsche's last men, for whom the absurdity of human life is a source of bemusement.

Renton leads us to the final stage of nihilism, but his attempted transcendence of consumerist life resists the complete conflation of nihilism and conventional society. The identification of the two is now a staple of television sitcoms, but it is nowhere more creatively or thoroughly explored than in the sitcom *Seinfeld*. In completing the devolution of nihilism in our popular culture, *Seinfeld* echoes not only *Trainspotting* but also the casual comedy of *Pulp Fiction*. The vignette structure of *Pulp Fiction* is similar to that of a situation comedy. It is instructive that Jerry Seinfeld sees similarities between *Pulp Fiction* and his own show: "I thought *Pulp Fiction* was very much in the tone of a lot of things we do. Some of that coffee-shop stuff between John Travolta and Sam Jackson—I thought, that's like a me-and-George scene."[1] Tarantino is himself an avowed *Seinfeld* fan.[2] His comment that *Pulp Fiction*'s characters are a "cross between criminals and actors and children playing roles" might also serve as an apt description of *Seinfeld*'s major characters, who have such a fragile sense of self that they are incapable of living any determinate form of life. Their unformed, childlike characters render them capable of slipping in and out of various roles, even the role of the criminal. In another similarity to *Pulp Fiction*, *Seinfeld* (more than any sitcom in history) makes ample, even excessive, use of comic coincidence. It thus raises the question of whether the author of the whole is a provident God or the dark, anti-provident power who has haunted humanity since the advent of modernity.

BEYOND THE DYSFUNCTIONAL FAMILY: *Seinfeld*

In linking *Seinfeld* to nihilism, I do not mean to reduce its remarkable success (Jay McInerny calls it the best comedy ever) to an implicit philosophical supposition. Like its successful predecessors, such as *The Honeymooners* and *I Love Lucy*, *Seinfeld* has well-defined characters with great comic range and extraordinary chemistry. Kramer and Elaine provide the sort of physical, slapstick humor that was a staple in shows like *Dick Van Dyke* and *I Love Lucy*. Few comedies have had better dialogue, particularly when it comes to sexuality. At a time when untalented entertainers go for the cheap laugh, *Seinfeld* excels at the art of suggestion through indirect locution.

As much as *Seinfeld* may have in common with previous comedies, its underlying nihilism entails a number of departures from its predecessors. Whereas the family supplied the dramatic and moral structure to the plot for earlier comedies, *Seinfeld* focuses almost exclusively on the lives of single individuals, for whom family life seems improbable, if not impossible. As the embodiment of American virtues, the family used to provide a framework for that most serious of American pursuits, the pursuit of happiness. These comedies were often didactic, sometimes blatantly so; they provided brief lessons on virtues such as thrift, fairness, compromise, honesty, and hard work. These are not heroic virtues, but rather those of the ordinary citizen, peculiarly American virtues whose lineage can be traced all the way back to Ben Franklin's *Autobiography*. Even where these sitcoms are not explicitly didactic, they still exude the confidence of the American spirit, its optimism and buoyancy, its belief in the fundamental reasonableness and justice of democracy, American style.

For these comedies, family life presents an endless array of comic situations, situations that remind us of our limitations, even of the limits of authority figures like teachers and parents. Of course, the foibles of authority figures are not the final word and the necessity for such figures is never really put in question. The sort of limitations revealed in this genre do not produce radical individualism; on the contrary, they serve to remind us of our need for one another, of our common predicament, possibilities and hopes, and vision of the good life. The main characters are flawed and imperfect persons, often muddling through, but they have enough clarity about their goals to distinguish what is important from what is not. The early sitcoms remind the audience of these things and invite their participation in our common American destiny. Laughter arises from shared vision and feeling. How different is this sort of laughter from the detached and mocking laughter in contemporary depictions of dysfunctional family life in shows like *The Simpsons* and *Married . . . with Children*?

For all their peculiarly American features, previous sitcoms have a basically classical comic structure to them. Most episodes of *I Love Lucy* revolve around some loony plan of Lucy's, which puts her in a seemingly insoluble situation. As viewers wonder how she will ever get out of the mess, their feelings of concern mix with an anticipation of the dilemma's resolution. Of course, viewers' expectations are never thwarted, disaster is always averted, Lucy hugs Ricky, and all is right with the world. The typical comedy presupposes sympathy on the part of the audience for the characters. We laugh *with* not *at* Lucy.

Seinfeld marks a decisive break from nearly all the conventions of the classic American comedy. Perhaps the easiest way to bring out the differences is to focus on *Seinfeld's* dethroning of the family. *Cheers* certainly anticipates *Seinfeld* in this. The families that do appear—Carla's, Fraser and Lillith, and especially Cliff and his mother—play none of the normalizing roles of families in previous sitcoms. They anticipate the dysfunctional families of 1990s sitcoms. Yet an important theme in *Cheers* was the relationship between Sam and Diane, and at some level the issue was always whether they would get married. Although there was much fodder for comedy in their impossible relationship, the tone was not finally comic, but that of the sorrowful sense of a possibility lost. Who can forget the maudlin final parting between Sam and Diane, with Sam alone in the bar whispering, "Have a good life"? Instead of banishing the family completely, *Cheers* replaces it with the bar, the place where everybody knows your name. *Cheers* is much too sentimental a comedy to fully dethrone the family.

Seinfeld is never sentimental. Outside of a small coterie of acquaintances, Jerry's world is one where very few persons know your name—and you wish that many of those who do know did not. On one occasion, Kramer nearly ruins Jerry's life by pasting named pictures of all the residents of their apartment building at its entrance. In another episode, Elaine's suggestion to the chief advisor of David Dinkens's mayoral campaign, that everyone in the city should wear a name tag so New York would be just like a small town, loses Dinkens the election. The family is cast in a similar light. Jerry's and George's parents represent a kind of conventionalized lunacy. There is barely a residue of the Sam and Diane relationship in Jerry and Elaine, and it is never really treated seriously. More characteristic is the episode in which they attempt to add sexual activity to their comfortable friendship.

In a world where the family is displaced, children can only be seen as aliens. They are something worse than that on *Beavis and Butt-Head* and *South Park*. On *Seinfeld*, children are rarely seen and ambivalence about their very existence is hilariously played out in the "vasectomy" episode. In order to attract women who are sure they do not want kids, nearly all the men decide to have vasectomies. Inevitably, the women change their minds. In an era of technological sexuality, cold calculation replaces romance and passion. In the episode in which Elaine's favorite contraceptive device, the sponge, goes off the market, she initiates a complicated "screening process," interviewing potential candidates to determine whether they are "sponge-worthy."

The dethroning of the family does not involve a radical critique of family or any sense that we could live wholly independent of connections of blood. This is a bit surprising, given that the location of the show is New York City, the twentieth-century Mecca for angst-ridden artists and rebels against bourgeois values. But rebellion presupposes a standard in light of which present power structures can be found wanting—or at least the presence of something that merits opposition. The advent of nihilism deprives the rebel both of worthwhile enemies and of a claim to moral superiority. The aspiration to radicalism becomes just as silly as the convention it seeks to undermine. Elaine occasionally adopts politically correct positions, but she either cannot sustain her commitment or looks utterly ridiculous. She anticipates the most controversial female character on current television, Ally McBeal, who invokes among women equally passionate responses of adulation and censure. Some see in her conflicted and vulnerable character a refreshingly honest depiction of the situation of contemporary women, torn between different, perhaps incompatible, conceptions of womanhood. Others see in her a regression from the strong, independent-minded model of the feminist. A *Time* magazine cover story entitled "Is Feminism Dead?" features Ally along with feminist icons like Gloria Steinham. The real problem is not with the character Ally, but with the world of *Ally McBeal*, a world in which the heroic and prophetic voice of feminist opposition is no longer credible. When asked about Ally's line, "I want to change the world; I just want to get married first," Calista Flockhart, who plays Ally, responded, "Being loved is a basic human need. Who wants to be alone?"[3] Yet love continues to elude Ally.

Like its chief contender for 1990s sitcom supremacy, *The Simpsons*, *Seinfeld* lacks both moralistic defenses and rebellious critiques of the family. The trivial aspirations of the family render it not so much above criticism as comically beneath it. Although *The Simpsons* is not so individualistic as *Seinfeld*, its uncanny combination of nihilism with familial sentimentality is in some ways more disturbing. *The Simpsons* illustrates what Tocqueville called the "naturalness" of the democratic family in the absence of the old hierarchical relations between parents, especially the father, and children. Familiarity, it turns out, simultaneously breeds affection and contempt. For the most part, Homer is one of the kids, who address him as they do their friends. When Marge thinks she may be pregnant again, Bart cheers his father: "Homer, you're a machine!" Nearly every episode contains a scene where Bart's acerbic wit provokes Homer into clutching his son's throat and yelling, "Why, you little . . . !" Homer embodies the return to a primitive, nearly sub-human state of nature. He is ruled by his appetites and inclinations, his desire for food, beer, sex, and get-rich schemes. He is capable of detached, malevolent humor at the expense of others; indeed, he often relishes these experiences with his son, Bart. In one episode, after being caught driving drunk, he is forced to attend driver's reform school and watch a gory video of accidents caused by drunk drivers. While others faint or throw up, Homer giggles: "It's funny because I don't know him." Yet he is also capable of affection and sympathy. Throughout, he is barely rational; in the face of the most powerful human experiences, he is typically inarticulate, responding to frustration with his trademark "D'oh!" or to grief or joy with a spontaneous moan.

Like the television screen around which the Simpsons gather to watch the violent cartoon *The Itchy and Scratchy Show*, the animated characters on *The Simpsons* are all surface. But the lack of depth, complexity, and mystery is not peculiar to animation. Think of the way *Ally McBeal* immediately reveals to the viewing audience the innermost feelings and thoughts of characters; lust is symbolized by an extended tongue, while Ally's fears that she is being dumped are expressed in the image of her being dropped into a huge trash can. What one critic says about *Seinfeld*'s characters can be easily generalized: "They only play at self-knowledge;

any real consciousness of who they are ... would be like the cartoon moment when Bugs Bunny looks down and realizes he's walking on air."[4]

The loss of depth leads to a blurring of the private and the public. The demise of the family and the attendant erosion of what Tocqueville calls intermediate institutions are also contributing factors. On the occasionally tragic but mostly melodramatic *ER*, the emergency room is the home and one's coworkers, family, as Dr. Mark Green, played by Anthony Edwards, explicitly notes in one episode. The ER is a kind of therapeutic forum to which individuals bring their baggage from past and present relationships and where new hopes feebly seek to displace former disappointments, only to suffer the inevitable failure of love's labor's lost. Similarly, on *Ally McBeal* the court is the arena for the working out of personal neuroses and tribulations of the heart. Even more telling is the way *Ally McBeal*'s unisex bathroom replaces the *Cheers* bar and *Seinfeld*'s coffee shop. It functions as a place for (public?) congregating, where needs, wants, insecurities, and conflicts are sometimes aired, at times provoked, and occasionally resolved. One actor from the show likens the bathroom to the "kitchen in most people's houses at parties." Another comments, "There's no place safe at that office. There's no privacy anywhere. You can get into a lot of trouble in that bathroom."[5]

Apologists for contemporary television often appeal to its realism—the predictable last line of defense for bankrupt artists. The older tradition of American sitcoms is often rightly criticized for its excessive sentimentality and its sanitized view of family life. The ease with which moral dilemmas were resolved and suffering overcome presupposed an artificial world, void of destructive sin and habitual vice. In spite of both artificiality and superficiality, these comedies were often quite effective at capturing the language and humor of children. Indeed, the shows embodied a clear distinction between the world of children and that of adults and never doubted the task of initiating the inhabitants of the former into the latter. But this distinction is now lost in American society and its television shows. In place of the realms of childhood and adulthood, there is the hybrid of perpetual adolescence. The goal is to have all the privileges of adult life with the lack of responsibility characteristic of childhood. The Puritan work ethic, which was still central to shows like *I Love Lucy* or even *The Brady Bunch*, is completely absent from *Seinfeld*, as it is from *The Simpsons*, whose characters expend enormous effort trying to avoid work. In response to Homer's complaint that striking teachers are trying "to pawn the kids off on their parents," the intellectually precocious Lisa explains the principled reasons for the strike. Homer counters, "That's not the way to handle things. You just go to work and do the same half-assed job every day."

Along with the demise of the family, *Seinfeld* exhibits skepticism about the pursuit of happiness. Early sitcoms depicted the family as the horizon of the pursuit of happiness and as the embodiment of the American dream. Over the years, sitcoms have seen an abridgment of ambition with respect to happiness and the American dream. *Seinfeld* represents the disappearance of this overarching pursuit as a major theme. Clearly there are anticipations of this in highly successful shows like *M*A*S*H*, which during its last years focused on the frustrations of the American aspiration for happiness and on the hypocrisy in the American claim to embody the best life available. Allan Alda's character, Hawkeye, became especially acerbic toward his country. But in its serious, almost tragic, depiction of the costs of war and in its consciously critical stance toward American life, $M^*A^*S^*H$ ranges over a number of genres and is therefore no longer merely a comedy. The abdication of pure comedy is an inevitable result of the attempt to treat serious issues seriously. It reflects the more somber, less confident tone of the post-1960s, post-Vietnam, post-Watergate America, a nation much more devoted to self-scrutiny and more afflicted by self-doubt than the nation of the 1950s.

Like much of end-of-the-century America, *Seinfeld* transcends such seriousness; unlike sitcoms from $M^*A^*S^*H$ through *Ellen*, it never gives in to the temptation to take itself seriously, and in this respect it returns us to pure comedy. Jerry Seinfeld traces his inspiration to the skits of Abbot and Costello, a form of comedy void of any interest in moral instruction or social critique. If *Seinfeld* returns to that original model of American comedy, it does so in unprecedented ways. Whereas the older pure comedies avoided serious issues at all costs and thus tended toward innocuous slapstick, the scope of *Seinfeld*'s humor is unlimited. All the grave topics, whose treatment turned other comedies tragic or at least melodramatic, are but additional subjects of comic insight for *Seinfeld*. The unlimited scope of *Seinfeld*'s humor is both a presupposition and a consequence of its nihilism.

The formerly revered American dream is now fragmented and makes its presence felt more in the form of occasionally deceptive nightmares. Characters are episodically gripped by a passion to find a kind of completion to their lives, to have it all, but this is nothing more than a fleeting and irrational passion, one among many possible temporary obsessions to which we are liable. This is the ironic flip-side to the pointlessness of life, an irony out of which *Seinfeld* has gotten much mileage. In a world without meaning, anything can become a source of absolute significance, or, more accurately, maniacal obsession, at least for a time. Irrational obsession is a dominant theme of *Seinfeld*. Kramer's whole life is consumed by a series of unrelated obsessions: driving a fire truck, hitting golf balls on the beach, or opening a restaurant where customers make their own pizza. Recall the show where Elaine develops an attachment to an unattractive and bizarre man precisely because he cannot remember her name.

The arbitrariness at the root of contemporary relationships and the obsessions that they breed are rich sources of comedy. The break-up is inevitable and is usually occasioned by something trivial, whether it be Elaine's indignation at a boyfriend's failure to write an exclamation point at the end of a message containing dramatic news, Jerry's work as a comic not being respected by his date (a cashier), or his attraction to a voluptuous woman being ruined by her man-like hands.

In a world where arbitrary, individual preferences rule, relationships can be nothing more than games, more or less sophisticated, more or less humorous. In one episode, Elaine is distraught that Kramer extended her regards to a guy she had recently dropped. When Elaine complains that Kramer's "unauthorized 'hi'" has lost her the "upper hand," Jerry comments that "it's like a game of tag." In another episode, Elaine falls for a professional mover who does not play games. Jerry says, "No games. What's the point of dating without games? How do you know if you're winning or losing?" The prominence of adolescent power struggles makes lying an indispensable art, an art for which George has "the gift." As he advises Jerry in one of the many "must-lie" situations on the show, "It's not a lie if you believe it."

THE DEATH OF MAN—AND WOMAN, TOO

In its subtle analysis of relationships, *Seinfeld* discerns something like Nietzsche's will to power. For him, the idea of an objective moral ideal is an illusion, a human construct. What is actually at the root of all our conscious life, underlying our division of actions into good and evil, is an unconscious and amoral force, the will to power. He prophesied the coming of a new age of humanity, embodied in the superman, who would emerge richer, stronger, more varied, from having lived through the transforming era of nihilism. Inspired by his deeply aristocratic sense of rank, Nietzsche's superman is an artist who harnesses the chaotic will to power in order to create new and nobler values. *Seinfeld*'s will to power knows no such grand aspiration. The preoccupation with power evinces the precarious, indeed illusory, character of freedom. Assertions of independence and control inevitably generate a reversal and lead to groveling submission. All the major characters at some point find themselves beholden to the manipulative and devious Newman, whose very name is spoken in a tone of utmost disdain. The Superman of Jerry and George is the comic-book figure, whose statue sits on Jerry's bookshelf. They admire him, not for his altruistic motives or sense of mission, the things that made him an American icon, but for his power. Their refashioned comic-book hero is thus also beyond good and evil, dangerously close to a combination of Superman and Bizarro Superman. Being closer to Nietzsche's last men than to his superman, they do not detect the danger. In spite of their voracious appetite for conversation, they are unable even to formulate their dilemma.

The amoral tone of much of the show's humor does not mean that there are no longer any rules. And the rules that continue to function in such a world are essentially comic. As usual, *Seinfeld* has seen this and put it to good use. Some rules have to do with the conventions of power, as in Elaine's game of tag with her former mate or Susan's insistence on the rule that couples tell one another everything. Other rules save us from embarrassment: when asked to comment about the appearance of an ugly baby, one must lie. Sometimes it is difficult to determine precisely what the rule is. How many dates after a sexual encounter must one endure before breaking with a partner? Lots of traditional moral rules are flouted and even where they have some force, as in obligatory attendance at funerals, nothing more than external conformity makes sense. Elaine spends her time at one funeral expressing her dissatisfaction with her attire. Most of the rules concern apparently trivial matters, such as George's claim that "airport pick-up is a binding social contract" or Kramer's insistence on the inviolable status of the rules constituting the etiquette of golf: "A rule's a rule and, let's face it, without rules there's chaos." The seemingly insignificant takes on a nonnegotiable status.

One may protest a rule but it is not really possible to evade it. After apparently having been caught picking his nose, Jerry denies culpability and then complains, "What's wrong with picking? Is it one of the ten commandments? Did God say thou shalt not pick?" In another episode, Jerry's protests against the obligatory day-after thank you earns him a rebuke from Kramer: "If you don't want to be part of society, why don't you get in your car and move to the East Side?"

Kramer learns the hard way about the status of such rules when AIDS walkers vilify and beat him for refusing to wear his AIDS ribbon.

Instead of the nihilistic era eliminating rules, initiating a lapse into a kind of anarchy, there is a medley of rules with no clear relationship to one another. There is something capricious and comical in the continuing hold that rules have on us; they operate like taboos, making little or no sense but nonetheless exercising an irresistible psychological pressure. *Seinfeld*'s insight into the odd ways rules now function in our lives is a remarkable bit of comic genius. Nothing illustrates better the Pyrrhic victory of radical individualism. We have successfully thrown off the encumbrances of authority and tradition only to find ourselves subject to new, more devious, and more intractable forms of tyranny. Classical liberalism thought that the most just form of government was one that recognized the natural and inalienable rights of human beings to self-determination. There was a kind of naïve faith in the ability of untutored individuals to choose for the best, to act on the basis of their long-term interests. The belief was that the only rules to emerge from such a system would be rules reasonably consented to by a reflective majority or by their duly elected representatives. But the advent of democratic nihilism renders dubious the assumption of a link between autonomous individual choice and reason, between the fleeting desires of the self and the self's long-term interests.

One episode in particular illuminates the absurd consequences of making an absolute out of choice, the result of which is the trivialization of all objects of choice. After watching the opening of a film in which the main character finds herself in a coma, Kramer decides he needs a living will to insure he will die with dignity. Contemplating the weighty choice of a proxy, he considers appointing Jerry, who assures him, "Believe me. If given the legal opportunity, I will kill you." He settles on Elaine, who accompanies him to the lawyer's office to consider various hypothetical situations for the ending of his life. For one situation—"You're eating but machines do everything else"—Elaine counsels, "I'd stick," and Kramer agrees: "Yeah. I could still go to the coffee shop." The problem is that the impetuous Kramer failed to watch the rest of the movie before setting off in search of the living will. When he returns to the video, he discovers that the woman comes out of the coma, and he informs Jerry: "I've changed my mind about the whole coma thing. . . . I'm up for it."

As one's vagrant inclinations change from moment to moment, so too does one's thinking about the big questions. The precariousness of one's present choices divests the ultimate issues of all significance. When one's life plan is subject to the unpredictable tyranny of chance events or evanescent passion, the hollow assertion of a dignity based in autonomy becomes fodder for the comedian. It is hard to find a better description of nihilism or of how a liberalism that rests upon the inviolable right of each individual to construct his own vision of reality naturally generates nihilism.

Seinfeld fulfills the prophetic pronouncements of philosophers from Nietzsche to Foucault about the imminent death of man, the vanishing of the determinate self. In so doing, *Seinfeld* provides its own spin on Nietzsche's doctrine of eternal recurrence. As we have noted, each character's sense of self is subject to a seemingly endless series of changes, and yet each remains unchanged. One of the show's writers has confessed that there is only one rule in the composition of the show: the characters must never learn from their experiences; they must forever be what they intrinsically and eternally are. Self-proclaimed postmodern writers often treat the aspiration for transcendence, for permanence or wholeness, as misguided; they cast off being for the sake of becoming. *Seinfeld* depicts the consequences of such a project. There is nothing but banal repetition and the experience of eternal recurrence as unending frustration.

Each character on *Seinfeld* has his or her individual limits, but these are not moral limits; they are more like the limits of one's personality or lifestyle. This is most pointedly illustrated in the episode where Jerry and George are suspected of being gay. They spend the entire episode vociferously denying the accusation and vigorously defending their heterosexuality. Yet after each denial, they feel compelled to add, "not that there's anything wrong with that." Like other conventions once thought to reflect a natural order, heterosexuality has become an inexplicable remnant from the past. Instead of the body as ensouled, as the locus for the reception and expression of meaning and intimacy, the body is now a neutral and mute collection of organs and parts. The parts can be manipulated to produce pleasure. In one episode, Elaine attributes her failure to persuade a homosexual to change "teams" to her limited access to the male "equipment." When George's mother surprises him and interrupts his self-stimulation, she objects to his treating his body like an "amusement park." The fixation on the body does not unveil any deeper significance; it blinds the characters to the complementarity of the sexes. *Seinfeld* matter-of-factly confirms Renton's revolutionary prophecy that we're heterosexual by default, that in one thousand years there will be no men and no women: "It's all about aesthetics and f—k all to do with morality." The mild, prime-time equivalent to Renton's prophecy is *Ally McBeal*'s famous unisex bathroom, the "heart and soul" of the show. And all of this confirms Tocqueville's worry that, in spite of our bold proclamations of individualism, the result of our insatiable pursuit of equality is homogeneity. The lead writer for *Ally McBeal*, David Kelley, remarks, "I cringe when people ask me how I write women characters. The truth is, I just write them the way I write men. I don't distinguish."[6]

Other episodes of *Seinfeld* illustrate the preeminence of lifestyle over morality. For example, Jerry pushes the limits of possibility in his attempt to execute the "roommate switch," to trade his relationship with his present girlfriend for one with her roommate. On George's advice, he suggests a *ménage à trois*, presuming one woman will be offended and the other intrigued. The strategy backfires when the proposal is accepted. But Jerry cannot go through with it because "I'm not an orgy guy." He would have to get orgy clothes, buy special oils, and so forth. When George attempts to extricate himself from a relationship with a woman who has a male roommate, he deploys the same *ménage à trois* strategy, thinking it will disgust her. When the woman turns to her roommate and excitedly informs him that George is "into" the *ménage*, we are left with the image of George's face in a silent, contorted scream reminiscent of the figure in Edvard Munch's painting *The Scream*.

Seinfeld's DARK GOD

The comparison with Munch's painting might seem inapposite, since that image is designed to induce in us a feeling of horror, not laughter. But the way Munch's image of horror has now made it into popular culture in the form of posters, coffee mugs, place mats, and even blow-up dolls, is an instructive confirmation of the nearly universal undermining of the grave by the light, the reversal of the tragic into the comic. We may not yet be used to thinking of the pointlessness of life as funny; we are more accustomed to the dreary, depressing angst of artists. *Seinfeld* keeps us laughing, and hence we fail to see its underlying nihilism. That we find it funny evinces the absence of sympathy, the disconnection, between audience and character. This is the same sort of disconnection that the characters on *Seinfeld* exhibit toward one another. We laugh as much *at* as *with* these characters.

Some fans thought the death of George's fiancée, Susan, who poisoned herself while licking envelopes for wedding invitations, was callous. It may not have been the most creative moment in the show, but nothing in the manner of the termination of that relationship was incongruous with the dominant kind of humor in the show. Her death was untimely only in the sense that it took so long for it to happen. The famous "Junior Mint" episode is also rife with callous humor. It closes with Kramer and Jerry observing a surgery from a booth above the operating table. Kramer, who has brought candy to increase his enjoyment of the performance, drops a Junior Mint right into the incision. Before agreeing to accompany Kramer to the hospital, Jerry hems and haws. Finally, he relents: "All right. Let's go watch them slice the fat bastard up." Seinfeld himself has called that line a turning point in the series.

The end of George's *ménage à trois* episode and Susan's death are but two of the many examples of *Seinfeld*'s art of the unhappy but comical ending. There is often something fitting in the way chance events conspire to undermine the hopes or aspirations of one or more of the characters, or, as in the case of Susan's death, in the way one person's tragedy is another's comedy. *Seinfeld* skillfully introduces and balances a number of seemingly unrelated plot lines and then brings them together at the end. The coincidence of events means that we can discern in life something more than mere unrelated chance, even if it does not lead us to apprehend some underlying principle of order in the way comedies of an earlier era do. Not just the endings of particular episodes, but other sorts of partings or separations are treated comically. Compare the melodramatic ending of the relationship between Sam and Diane on *Cheers* with the nonchalant ending of Jerry's engagement, where both blurt out "I hate you" and then casually wish each other well. Lots of shows, for example, *ER*, highlight the frustration of human affection, the way the circumstances of our times thwart the very possibility of love. But to maintain a straight face, let alone a stiff upper lip, in the face of meaninglessness is difficult. Nihilism mocks such gravity. If there is nothing beyond me in light of which I might understand myself and appraise my actions and goals, then how is any particular course of action more worthy of choice than any other? If meaninglessness is the ultimate framework, then what's the point of striving at all? What's all the fuss about? If *ER* comes close to tragedy in its poignant depiction of the inescapable futility of the search, *Ally McBeal*'s penchant for the absurd, for portraying the pursuit of love as a kind of farce, tends toward the comic. But Ally cannot quite relinquish the quest. In a maudlin and mildly self-deceiving tone, she muses at the end of the inaugural episode that she really does not want to be content. That would mean the end of the quest, which she prefers to the catch because the "more lost you are, the more you have to look forward to." The implication? She must "be happy and just not know it."

The abdication of the quest, or at least of any real possibility for its fulfillment, is both a cause and a consequence of the deprivation of the self. *Seinfeld*'s world is populated by Nietzsche's last men, who, when faced with the great questions and ultimate issues of life, blink and giggle. In a world with no ultimate sense of good and evil or of shared purpose, taking a moral stance is inevitably construed as striking a pose. The point is hilariously played out in the show about abortion, where Jerry first instigates a near riot at Poppie's restaurant by bringing up the matter and then nips in the bud Elaine's affection for a man by inquiring where he stands on the issue. The shrill and indignant tone of the verbal battle at Poppie's captures the character of public debate in a nihilistic world, or rather of the impossibility of having a public debate about fundamental issues. In the same episode, Kramer enlists Poppie's support for his idea of a pizza shop where customers make their own pizza. The cooperative venture is quickly doomed by a debate over whether individuals should be given the right to choose whatever topping they wish. Poppie objects and insists, "On this topic there can be no debate." The argument shifts to the controversial question of when a pizza becomes a pizza. When you first put your hands into the dough or not until it comes out of the oven? On the surface, the exchange mocks both sides in the abortion debate, but the underlying motif is that of morality as farce. There is no higher or lower. Pizza, abortion—it's all the same.

The classic American sitcom presupposed both an order of higher and lower and a shared vision of America as providing the best framework for the pursuit of a good human life. As I noted earlier, in spite of the notable absence of explicit attention to religious themes, the original television sitcoms embodied a civic religion and their ability to bring events to a happy ending was a kind of justification of American democracy. In this genre, the happy ending is usually brought about through an unanticipated event. Whereas in the classic tragedy, an almost cosmic necessity leads to the downfall of the hero, in a comedy chance or coincidence is the key to the culmination of the action. Tragedy, in Aristotle's definitive formulation, achieves its emotional effect by inducing in the audience feelings of pity and fear for the fallen hero. If comedy arouses those feelings at all, it does so somewhere near the beginning of the action, when it leads the characters into apparent harm. But the light-hearted tone of comedy invites the audience to see through the apparent injury and to anticipate its resolution.

Through a chance event, apparent evils and seeming dilemmas are averted. Since a chance event interrupts the flow of the action, it might seem to render the drama incoherent or implausible. Yet, since it brings about a happy ending and usually leads the major characters to put any enmity aside and reconcile themselves to one another and to a fate that is better than their behavior merits, the power behind the coincidence is benevolent. The role of chance in comedy engenders in the audience a spirit of wonder and gratitude, wonder because the benevolent orchestration of human events surpasses our immediate comprehension, gratitude because our destiny surpasses our merits.

Given this account of chance or coincidence in traditional comedy, it might seem that *Seinfeld* is not so novel as I have proposed, since it is replete with coincidences. Indeed, it makes use of coincidence as a structuring principle much more than any other comedy of which I am aware. What are we to make of the prominent role of coincidence in *Seinfeld*? One possibility is that *Seinfeld* deploys coincidence as *mere* coincidence, not as opening up the possibility of perceiving some higher order of intelligibility. Many episodes do indeed leave us with simply a series of coincidences. When these coincidences seem to serve a harmonious end, the goodness or order they bring about is not that of a higher or comprehensive sort. In one episode, Jerry regrets having arranged for Elaine to move into the apartment above him, a move that would curb his independence and unduly complicate his sex life. When he learns that someone else has offered five thousand dollars up front for the rent-controlled apartment and that Elaine is in no position to make a counteroffer, he rejoices. Then he waxes philosophical and confides to George that he used to think that the universe was just a series of unrelated occurrences; he now realizes that there is "reason and purpose to everything." For Jerry order in the universe is indistinguishable from chance conspiring to satisfy his preferences.

In most episodes, however, chance events seem ordered to a malevolent end. Instead of coincidence operating as a sign of a benign providential order beyond our comprehension, it functions as a kind of anti-providence. Even when the conclusion is "fortunate," it does not bring all the parties to a better state. In fact, this is true of the episode just cited, where Jerry's luck coincides with Elaine's loss of the apartment. The good luck of some is purchased at the cost of misery for others. The most humorous illustration of this principle is in the episodes focusing on Kramer's attempt to find himself by traveling to California. Kramer's bad luck, which begins with his car breaking down on the freeway, reaches its nadir when he is charged with being the "smog killer" after the woman he had been dating is found murdered with a piece of paper on her person bearing Kramer's name. For a while things look bad for Kramer. Luckily, so to speak, there is another murder while he is in jail. As Jerry, George, and Kramer jump up and down joyfully chanting that the smog killer has struck again, a family, palpably in mourning, passes them and enters the police station. Even after all this, Kramer considers staying in California. To Jerry's incredulity at his plans and objection that nothing good has happened since he arrived in LA, Kramer responds "I met a girl." Jerry again objects: "Kramer, she was murdered!" And Kramer answers: "I wasn't looking for a long-term relationship."

There is explicit evidence of this line of thinking in a number of episodes. Recall, for example, the show about the pilot Jerry and George have submitted to NBC. At one point, the pilot's acceptance looks highly likely, yet George is increasingly paranoid about a discoloration on his lips. Of course, everyone he bumps into, including an Arab cab driver, comments on the discoloration and suggests he get it checked out. Confident that his demise is near, George complains to Jerry: "God will never let me enjoy success." Jerry queries: "I thought you didn't believe in God," to which George responds, "For the bad things I do." In another episode, already mentioned, Jerry all-knowingly informs Elaine that the only reason she is pursuing a certain man is that he cannot remember her name. Shaken from self-oblivion, she states, "That's sick." Jerry dispassionately explains that "it's God's plan. He doesn't really want anyone to get together."

Although much of *Seinfeld* testifies to the death of God,

it also lends credence to the view that God is alive and well—just indistinguishable from the devil. This is precisely the sort of God that would account for the social world of *Seinfeld*, a world constructed around a set of arbitrary and unavoidable rules. *Seinfeld*'s God is a capricious, whimsical, detached, and perhaps malevolent deity. *Seinfeld*'s God is identical to the hypothetical being that Descartes seeks to vanquish. Recall that this is "not a God, who is the supreme source of truth, but a certain evil spirit, not less clever and deceitful than powerful, [who] has bent all his efforts to deceive me." This is not a God with whom we could enter into a social contract, let alone a biblical covenant. It is not even a God that we should reasonably fear; for, although he is all-powerful and has our fate in his hands, he is so unpredictable that our animosity or indifference is just as likely or unlikely to be efficacious as is our devoted obeisance.

This supreme being replaces not only the just and merciful God of the Judeo-Christian tradition, but also the intermediate, complacent all-American God. *Seinfeld* has seen through the modern American dream of blissful, uninterrupted leisure. Instead, leisure is tedious and the human condition is, as Pascal observed centuries ago, characterized by "boredom, inconstancy, and anxiety." *Seinfeld*'s comic nihilism divests Pascal's sobering insight of its tragic implications. Human life is a kind of game orchestrated by an indifferent or malevolent supreme being, whose desires we cannot assuage and whose power we cannot finally resist. We are not, however, entirely without recourse. We may not be made in the image and likeness of a good and rational God, but we can still imitate the divine by cultivating a comic detachment from the spectacle of human life.

PROMETHEUS AS ONAN

For most of the characters on *Seinfeld*, the prominence and function of coincidence serves to point toward the inevitability of their ultimate misery, of their being tricked yet again by Descartes's evil genius. Yet Jerry has a peculiar knack for avoiding such misery, especially in sexual relationships, where he is capable of an unrivaled detachment and indifference. Since happiness with others is not possible, it can be achieved only through a kind of comfortable isolation from others. If George has the gift of lying, Jerry has the gift of innate superficiality.

Given the nihilistic culture he inhabits, Jerry's detachment is both prudent and a source of free entertainment. He boasts to George that the uproar over abortion in Poppie's restaurant was pretty much all his fault Of course, Jerry's comic take on nihilism requires a kind of Stoic distance. It also requires luck. Jerry has both. Like the other characters, he can succumb to little obsessions or passions, most notably when he learns that Elaine never had an orgasm while they were dating. Yet, generally speaking, his detachment is greater than that of any other character. Fortune also shines on him: he is, as Kramer calls him, "even Steven." He relishes the way everything balances out for him while the fortunes of his friends are dashed.

Jerry comes closer than anyone else on the show to achieving perpetual adolescence, except of course when his career as a professional comedian is at issue. He does care about his success as a comedian, success that he cannot achieve without the assistance of others. His professional life has complications and frustrations—whether these be in the form of an inept agent or a harassing audience—that his personal life lacks. When it comes to work, Jerry must emerge from the adolescent self-absorption that is a central motif of *Seinfeld*. The aspiration for adulthood is a residual social and psychic artifact, capable of resurfacing almost at any time and catching one unawares. The famous episode where Jerry and George decide to get married begins with the two of them in the coffee shop lamenting their immaturity. "We're like children. . . . We're not men. . . . We come up with all these reasons to break up with women. We're pathetic. . . . It would be nice to care about someone." They make a deal to pursue serious relationships. As George enthusiastically runs off to convince Susan that he's ready to make a commitment, Jerry is saved from such a disastrous course of action by some timely advice from Kramer. When Jerry relates their conversation and resolution to Kramer, he knowingly responds: "So, you asked yourself—isn't there something more to life? Let me clue you into something. There isn't." Kramer proceeds in rich detail to demonstrate his thesis that marriage is a man-made prison. Bolstered by Kramer's advice, Jerry breaks with Melanie because she "eats her peas one at a time."

If marriage is Hell and relationships are traps, then being alone would seem to be an ideal. In one episode, Jerry comments that a walking date is good because there's not a lot of "face-to-face" contact. Elaine adds "it's the next best thing to being alone." Isolation involves an abridgment of one's sexual ambitions, or at least of one's sense of sexual conquest, but it by no means entails the elimination of sexual satisfaction. In many respects, autoerotic activity is superior to sexual congress with another, since it involves none of the complications attendant upon the latter. The experience of pure sex, of having sex as one wants it, without all the un-welcome human elements that accompany interaction with others, is the impossible dream of *Seinfeld*. Recall the show where Jerry and Elaine, disappointed at their lack of pros-pects in things genital, hit upon the idea that they could satisfy their needs through one another. Anticipating com-plications, they introduce certain rules of conduct, for ex-ample, staying over is optional and no calling the day after sex. That the experiment is obviously doomed from the outset confirms C. S. Lewis's insight that "lust is more ab-stract than logic."

The famous "master of your domain" episode underscores the essential role of masturbation in the world of *Seinfeld*. The contest to see who can go the longest without mastur-bating (won, surprisingly, by George) is provoked by George's relating how his mother had unexpectedly come home to find him, as she puts it, treating his body "like an amuse-ment park." So shocked is she by her discovery that she falls and injures herself. When George visits her in the hospital, she remarks, "Too bad you can't do that for a living. . . . You could sell out Madison Square Garden. Thousands of people would come to watch you. You could be a big star."

AMERICA AS A SEMIOTIC HELL

The America of *Seinfeld* is, as America always has been, the land of endless possibility, the only country founded on the natural right to the pursuit of happiness. But there are no frontiers left to conquer, just fleeting appetites and residual desire for fulfillment. Still, we cannot seem to shake off the language of our history, the language of individual rights, of human dignity, of equality, and of success and happiness. We are trapped in a semiotic Hell, of which there is no clear diagnosis and from which there can be no escape. The situation would be tragic, were we capable of sustained gravity and were it not so absurd.

In addition to being one of most humorous examples of a show without a plot, the episode entitled "The Parking Garage" is a splendid metaphor for the vision of human life as a world of apparent signs, symbols, and guideposts leading nowhere. On a trip to a Jersey mall, where Kramer has purchased an air conditioner, and Elaine, some tropical fish, the gang misplaces the car in the mall's parking garage. Unable to reach any consensus on where they came in, they trade guesses on which color, number, or level the car is located. All the signs begin to merge. Grasping their existential dilemma, George comments, "We're like rats in some experiment." The indifference of others to their plight is evident in Elaine's repeated failures to enlist anyone's assistance in finding their car. After appealing to their sense of compassion—one passerby frankly admits to her that he would not get any satisfaction out of helping them—she adopts a different strategy: "I can understand your not caring about us, we're human, but what about the fish?" The problem is that animal rights activists do not hang out at malls in New Jersey.

After they all become separated, Elaine, Jerry, and George are reunited and fortuitously find the car. Their good luck is but momentary, since Kramer, the driver, is not with them. By the time he arrives, Elaine's fish have died. Fittingly, the exhausted crew suffers a final humiliation when the car will not start. We have here of course yet another example of the unhappy but humorous ending. What we can now say about that structure is that it reflects the comic anti-providence of a world governed by a malevolent deity.

The sense of being trapped in a semiotic Hell is made explicit in the much-hyped final episode. When Jerry and George receive word that their five-year-old pilot has been picked up by NBC, they suppose that their dreams have been realized and begin to plan their move to California. NBC then calls to offer Jerry and his friends use of a network private jet to travel wherever they want. Soon after they leave on a flight for Paris, the plane is forced to make an emergency landing when Kramer tries to clear water from his ear and ends up crashing into the control panels in the cockpit. During what they think will be a short stay in a small Massachusetts town, they witness a car-jacking. As they make sarcastic remarks about the fat driver's misfortune, Kramer captures the moment on video. Soon a policeman arrives and arrests them for having violated a newly enacted Good Samaritan law. The prosecutor makes character the key issue and marshals some eighteen witnesses—a reunion of the most colorful characters to have appeared in the series—to demonstrate a "pattern of anti-social behavior." He promises that they will pay this time. After the jury returns a guilty verdict, the judge scolds them for behavior that "has rocked the very foundations" of society. The ending confirms Newman's prophecy from the opening of the episode; when Jerry refuses to let him tag along to Paris, he warns Jerry that his "day of reckoning is coming," that his "play world" will be shattered and the "smug smile" wiped off his face.

The excessive attention lavished on the show and its stars in the weeks leading up to last episode calls to mind Geoffrey O'Brien's remark: "Where it might once have been asked if *Seinfeld* was a commentary on society, the question now should probably be whether society has not been reconfigured as a milieu for commenting on *Seinfeld*."[7] Of course, that wry observation speaks volumes about our society, as does *Seinfeld* itself. Amid the mindless adulation before and after the finale, some critics issued jeremiads against the show's celebration of baby boomer self-absorption. This is true but superficial, reflecting the shallow moralism of boomer pundits. Others saw the last episode as a moral judgment on the characters.

Neither the detractors nor the boosters are on the mark. There is, as we have noted, a heavy dose of moralism in the episode, perhaps too much to be taken seriously. One problem is that Newman, the most diabolical person in the series, remains free. Moreover, it is not clear that conventional society or the justice system is much better off than are the characters on trial. Finally, it is simply not the case that up until now they have gotten away with their petty indulgences in the seven deadly sins. The thwarting of their attempt to escape their New York lives and capture the America dream in California is but the final confirmation that there is no way out for them. Whenever they think they are escaping, they run into themselves. Their lives in prison are essentially the same as they were outside. Jerry's biggest adjustment is the alteration of his cereal eating habits, while Elaine is anxious about having to wear an orange uniform. They have simply traded the coffee shop for the prison. To Jerry's observation that the second button on George's shirt is in the wrong place, George responds "haven't we had this conversation before?" They are destined to eternal recurrence.

CONCLUSION

Children of a Lesser God

IN HIS BOOK *The Plain Sense of Things*, James Edwards argues that nihilism is now our normal condition: "we are all now nihilists," leading "lives constituted by self-devaluing values."[1] Our cultural pathology is a "hangover from our religious and philosophical history." It is not just that we have yet to find the truth, but that the notion of truth itself is now thoroughly problematic. The guiding image for where we are now is the "regional shopping mall," where living becomes a matter of lifestyle choices for "rootless consumers." The most obvious danger is the "triumph of the normal," where normal is understood as a life of accumulation and entertainment. An opposite danger is that of pursuing "novelty for its own sake," arising from a restlessness that always wants to be anywhere but here.[2] Edwards thinks we can avert these two dangers by fostering social practices that cultivate the perception and imaginative appreciation of our forms of life. These are not absolute, unrevisable truths, but contingently constitutive features of

173

who we are. Even in this contingency, there is a degree of necessity, since who we are is never simply a matter of preference or choice. The ineluctability of our starting points and of the horizon of our options constrains without eliminating our freedom. But we still need sacraments, epiphanies that crystallize our experience of the world from our contingent perspective. For guidance, we can turn to poets like Wallace Stevens who train our imagination to ponder the "plain sense of things."[3]

If one objects that Edwards's hopeful note is groundless, his response is, "Precisely." If nihilism means anything, it is that there is no basis—religious, philosophical, or political—for confirming the truth of any position whatsoever; there is only the shifting ground of our history and experience. We will simply have to judge whether his remedy suits our history and our experience. If it does, we can implement the strategies he suggests and see what sort of life emerges. But if one looks at the way nihilism plays itself out in our popular culture, Edwards's suggestions seem naïve. Even at the level of philosophy, Edwards's position is an odd mix; he accepts Nietzsche's radical analysis of our times, but wants to forestall the devastating consequences Nietzsche thinks flow from it. Edwards gives us conservative nihilism. As a cultural analyst, he gets much right, especially concerning the dangers of our situation. But his own recommendations sound remarkably academic and theoretical, abstracted from the conditions he wishes to help shape.

The contrast with Nietzsche is instructive. Where Nietzsche emphasizes alternately the ennobling, tragic confrontation with nothingness and the affirming laughter of the value-creating soul, Edwards is somber and restrained, modest and joyless. The idea of a sacrament, without its vivifying source, the religious sacrifice, is an empty husk. Secular sacraments foster the bad faith of those who want the aesthetics of religion without its dogmatic, moral, and transcendental burdens. Edwards would give us a new civil religion to clothe the naked public square; the problem is that the square is already populated with demonic heroes. Nietzsche sees more clearly the great confrontation between his anti-Christ and the Judeo-Christian tradition. How much of popular culture is but a dramatic and violent inversion of the Gospel of peace, an immersion in sado-masochistic sex and impersonal egoism? As Walker Percy observes, we are living in the "dread latter days of the old violent beloved U.S.A. and of the Christ-forgetting Christ-haunted death-dealing Western world."[4]

In his perceptive study of contemporary popular culture, *Nightmare on Main Street: Angels, Sadomasochism, and the Gothic*, Mark Edmundson persuasively argues that ours is not the age of chaos that many decry and others celebrate. Instead, it is "shot through with a significant dialectical pattern," a conflict between the Gothic and the genre of "facile transcendence." Under the rubric of the Gothic, Edmundson locates phenomena as apparently diverse as the contemporary horror film, afternoon talk shows, and the O. J. Simpson trial. Among the salient features of the Gothic are a thorough critique of conventional authority, a preoccupation with revenge plots, with the unrelenting and disproportionate punishment of even the most minor of sins or flaws, and an obsession with the supernatural, especially in the form of haunting and possession. Facile transcendence, found in films like *Forrest Gump*, the self-help movement, and even the revival of Jane Austen, dismisses the Gothic as juvenile and embodies the hope of an easy way out of contemporary confusion.

Edmundson thinks that the primary reason for our contemporary preoccupation with the Gothic has to do with the cultural decline of religion. There is, I think, more to this remark than he realizes. An argument can be made that the artistic power of the Gothic and the Romantic is in some measure derivative of a Judeo-Christian worldview. This is, of course, a Nietzschean claim. In fact, Edmundson concedes and laments that ours is a "debased Gothic." We have its emphasis on haunting, on crime and punishment, without its counterbalancing accent on regeneration. Our Gothic resembles nothing so much as a dismembered *Divine Comedy*. It is equivalent to Dante's inferno without any prospect of purgatory or paradise, a world of unrelenting punishment which is the work not of a just and merciful God but of a malevolent and arbitrary force.[5]

Edmundson believes that the Gothic is composed of a set of dichotomies: between surface and depth, appearance and reality, and ego and id. Although Freud is now passé, Edmundson makes a persuasive case for the lingering influence of Freudian language on our discourse. Certainly there is a residual presence of Freudian language, but one wonders how much resonance it has. Few, if any, contemporary productions are more preoccupied with tracing out the roots and significance of sexual desire than is *Seinfeld*, but the quest leads to no great insight or self-knowledge, not even to terror. From *Seinfeld* to *Ally McBeal* to *The Simpsons*, characters are all surface, no depth. (The same case could be made for *Frasier*, an explicitly Freudian sitcom.) This is also the case with our contemporary heroes who stand beyond good and evil and seek to unmask the illusions of conventional morality. But the amoral hero substitutes surface for surface, since the notion that evil has depth is itself an illusion. Evil is revealed as banal. If there is a secret truth, it is that there is no truth. What these narratives retain is a shape, a pattern, a structure, and so the question about the unifying power or author of the story inevitably arises. Thus does the dark God come continually to the fore in contemporary popular culture. We moderns sometimes fancy ourselves beyond the crude and superstitious visions of an inscrutable, avenging divinity. An analysis such as Edmundson's belies that confidence.

Edmundson is nonetheless unwilling to investigate further the theological dimensions of our current culture. He may be right that the religious element is too often "intolerant and literal-minded,"[6] but his dismissal of the possibility of a religious response is sweeping and dogmatic and deprives him of an important conceptual resource. The contemporary fascination with angels (or the continuing popularity of the *Star Wars* series) is a feeble attempt to recover some of the elements of older comic narratives where heaven and earth combine to overcome the powers of darkness. The loss here is not just religious but human as well. Accompanying the decline in grand, providential narratives (or even the more tentatively affirmative narratives in film *noir*) is the shrinking and flattening of the world of man: the exaltation of the human ends in its debasement.

Without an all-powerful God to rebel against, even the devil cannot be taken seriously. The entire situation becomes comical, and yet we are unable to kill the divine. Like some resilient serial killer, God keeps popping back up. This, too, is a rather Nietzschean point: that wherever there are unifying cultural forces at work, there is a divinity present. The most patently deconstructive elements in Nietzsche aim at undercutting the possibility of a return to Judeo-Christian monotheism. This is a daunting task, as Nietzsche himself acknowledged: "We haven't rid ourselves of God because we haven't rid ourselves of grammar." What sort of deity do we now have?

In a famous eighteenth-century dialogue on religion, the skeptic David Hume mounts a sustained attack on the traditional conception of God as an infinitely perfect being. He sardonically suggests the following substitute: "[The universe is the] first rude essay of some infant deity, who afterwards abandoned it, ashamed of his performance; it is the work of some dependent, inferior deity, and is the object of derision to his superiors."[7]

In contemporary popular culture, we are the children of this lesser God, as is perhaps most evident in *The X-Files*. The show features Dana Scully and Fox Mulder as FBI agents in charge of investigating unsolved cases involving unexplained phenomena. By pairing these two, the FBI hopes that Scully's demand for scientific proof, cultivated during her training as a forensic pathologist, will temper Mulder's passion, inspired by his youthful witness of his sister's abduction by aliens, for unraveling the government cover-up of alien infiltration of the planet. Despite their different backgrounds and inclinations, Mulder and Scully forge an alliance, a friendship that transcends a prurient, even romantic, interest in one another. Whatever *eros* there is in their relationship is sublimated into the search for truth. The quest—encapsulated in the show's motto "the truth is out there"—imposes an ascetical restraint, a willingness to sacrifice personal well-being and success. It also demands truthfulness, at least toward those who assist us in the search.

Truth proves not only elusive but contradictory. What at one moment seems innocent or trustworthy can, and usually does, turn corrupt and insidious the next. One critic sees the show as a metaphor for humanity in the technological age of television. Scully and Mulder are

> literally and figuratively alienated, penetrated, and probed to the molecular level by omniscient and omnipotent forces who have infiltrated like television and, now, computers, virtually everything in our lives. . . . Scully and Mulder trust each other. . . . Yet virtually everything they think they know is wrong. Television has taught them the arts of insight but not how to formulate a point of view. It has sent them on a quest for identity, but taught them also never to trust what they find . . . . The media-driven milieu of *The X-Files* suggests that the whole world is now the same place, all of it accessible, all of it at once safe, dangerous, restricting, liberating. The North Pole is not more or less threatening than the New Jersey woods or a cheap motel room.[8]

The persistent plot reversals and illusory characters render the quest for truth problematic. The "truth is out there" competes for lead billing with other slogans like "trust no one" and "believe the lie."

The series tends to reverse and thereby unsettle traditional stereotypes; for example, the woman plays the hardheaded realist, while the man is credulous. But Scully and Mulder are less antithetical than complementary. Even before Scully shows signs of sharing Mulder's faith, the show illustrates the subtle link between skepticism and credulity in the absence of any clear basis for preferring one to the other. As Tocqueville notes, the confrontation with implacable, cosmic forces deprives the individual of a sense of control over his own life. The result is psychic inertia. Amid incessant investigative activity and in the face of the most horrifying revelations, both Scully and Mulder retain an almost icy detachment. *Entertainment Weekly* notes Scully's "open, blank stare" and Mulder's "pin-eyed zombie cool." There is something oddly mesmerizing and consoling about the conspiratorial artistry of the show. The experience of one's personal history, perhaps of the history of humankind, as the effect of the malevolent stratagems of some grand experiment conducted by aliens, the government, or some amalgam of the two (the Syndicate) induces a universal paranoia that has an inoculating quality.

Despite its *noir*ish elements, *The X-Files* often serves up a comical and satirical take on its fanciful theories, even on the quest for truth, thus providing further confirmation of the comic trajectory of contemporary treatments of evil. If there is a grand narrative to the series—and the revelations in the recent film and subsequent television episodes point rather strongly in that direction—it has to do with an alien plot to reclaim the earth. The planet's original inhabitants had a crucial hand in the evolution of the human species. Something slightly more than sci-fi escapism, this theory is regularly bandied about on the most popular late-night radio talk-show in the entire country, the *Art Bell Show*. The theory is the perfect mixture of theological myth and modern science. Thus do the apparently opposed tendencies toward skepticism and credulity converge.

The thesis of alien intervention in human evolution addresses (in mythological terms, of course) a quandary in which evolutionary theory now finds itself. The orthodox Darwinian view repudiates any rapid leap from one species to another. Darwin himself thought the appeal to quick alterations inexplicable, akin to the religious appeal to miracles. The incremental change that Darwin proposes as the mechanism of evolution requires an enormous amount of time; the worry is that not even the defeat of creationist suppositions about the novelty of the universe supplies a sufficient amount. Conversely, recourse to mutation, which creates what Stephen Jay Gould once called "hopeful monsters," also seems statistically implausible. Whatever may be the status of contemporary evolutionary theory (and it is not my intention here to impugn evolution itself), it tends to be unsatisfying to the popular mind, which has difficulty conceiving of human reasoning and aspiration as but the latest offshoot of a chance, mechanical process. The lesser God of Hume's dialogue, who is indistinguishable from the superhuman aliens of *The X-Files* and *The Art Bell Show*, is a fitting compromise between traditional religion and evolutionary theory, a myth for the new age.

The fragility of identity in the world of *The X-Files* often centers around the family. Yet, as one observer notes, families "scarcely matter except as plot devices." Perhaps what is more important, the question of family identity is always backward (toward uncovering the truth about the death of Scully's sister, about who abducted Scully and rendered her infertile, about the disappearance of Mulder's sister, and the relationships of his father and mother to less than savory individuals associated with the government conspiracy) and never forward (toward the possibility of marriage and child-rearing). As is often the case in film and on television, in *The X-Files* the family is a microcosm. In both the global and the local narratives, there is a desperate longing to recover what has vanished: a sense of belonging, of trust and stability. Both the cosmos, wherein human life issues from genetic manipulation by alien life forms, and the family, which is now at cross-purposes with itself, have suffered a cataclysmic blow which we seem unable to rectify or even to name clearly. How can we go on in a universe where the only thing that is trustworthy in the end is the insubstantiality, the nothingness, of what is most important and most personal, most universal and most immediate?

In our current culture no clear answer suggests itself. We have, admittedly, noted exceptions to the strong nihilistic bent of popular culture, and more could certainly be adduced. And although we have traced nihilism in culture through three stages (from the pursuit of evil through the banality of evil to normal nihilism as comic), nothing in our argument precludes the possibility of the emergence of narratives that encompass rather than fall prey to nihilism. Indeed, the sense of impending cataclysm has given rise to some of the most profound and ennobling dramas in our history. It is no coincidence that the best recent film treatments of the human confrontation with evil have been historical, for example, *Schindler's List* and *Malcolm X*. We shall certainly have to do a better job of cultivating memory, of fostering, as T. S. Eliot puts it, a sense of the presence of the past.

But here we must face the problem of culture itself, at least when it is understood as mere human construct. The cultivation of memory, of our link to the past, is now not something that comes naturally to us. It takes conscious effort, and, given the options, it is an onerous task which can too easily be seen as constricting of our freedom. The deeper problem with our culture is this: the most hip, the most clever, and the most humorous films and television series are laced with references to popculture itself, as if there were no world beyond that culture. This is as true in Quentin Tarantino's films and the *Scream* movies as it is in *Seinfeld*, *The X-Files*, and *The Simpsons*. If works of art do not allow the sort of self-awareness that suggests ways of transcending the world we have made, the givenness of convention, then all we are left with is an impotent self-consciousness. If everything is artifice, with no intelligible guiding purpose behind it, the very notion of nature becomes inconceivable and there is nothing independent of conventions and preferences to which we might appeal. Art narcissistically turns in on itself, unable to provide any insight into an order not of its own devising. Such a conception of culture easily reduces to an understanding of human life in terms of aesthetic self-creation, the Nietzschean problematic with which we began and whose nihilistic tendencies I have detailed. In this sense, the omnipresent lesser God can be seen as yet another construct, made in our image and likeness.

The spectacle of the self-canceling insights of self-made humanity is by turns amusing, captivating, enervating, and horrifying. Dare we add, instructive?

Notes

Introduction: Beyond Good and Evil

1 See Timothy Egan, "From Angst to School Killings," *The New York Times*, 14 June 1998, 1; and Mike Pearson, "The Price American Society is Paying for Violent Films," *The Washington Times Weekly Edition*, 20-26 April 1998, 36.

2 New York: HarperCollins, 1992.

3 For a recent and careful summary of the literature on this topic, see Allen D. Hertzke, "The Theory of Moral Ecology," *The Review of Politics* 60 (Fall 1998): 629-659.

1 Nihilism, American Style

1 New York: Avon Books, 1992.

2 *The Portable Nietzsche*, trans. Walter Kaufmann (New York: Viking Press, 1954), 129-30.

3 Friedrich Nietzsche, *Beyond Good and Evil*, trans. Walter Kaufmann (New York: Vintage Books, 1966), #201.

4 *Beyond Good and Evil*, #225.

5 Nietzsche, *The Will to Power*, trans. Walter Kaufmann (New York: Vintage Books, 1967) #125.

6 *Beyond good and Evil*, #13.

7 *The Will to Power*, #32.

8 *The Will to Power,* #9.

9 *The Will to Power,* #22.

10 Roger Shattuck, *Forbidden Knowledge: From Prometheus to Pornography* (New York: St. Martin's Press, 1996), 227-99.

11 Ibid., 280.

12 *The Will to Power,* # 2.

13 Ibid., #4.

14 Ibid., #12.

15 Ibid., #55.

16 Ibid., #15.

17 Ibid., #55.

18 See Peter Berkowitz, *Nietzsche: The Ethics of an Immoralist* (Cambridge: Harvard University Press, 1995).

19 Alexis de Tocqueville, *Democracy in America* (Anchor Books), Author's Preface to volume I.

20 See Nicholas Christopher, *Somewhere in the Night: Film Noir and the American City* (New York: The Free Press, 1997); and J. P. Telotte, *Voices in the Dark: The Narrative Patterns of Film Noir* (Urbana: University of Illinois Press, 1989).

21 *Somewhere in the Night,* 20.

22 *Voices in the Dark,* 17, 86.

23 Ibid., 87.

24 Ibid., 220-22.

25 Nietzsche, *The Genealogy of Morals,* trans. by F. Golffing (New York: Anchor Books, 1956), 191.

26 Cornell West, *Race Matters* (New York: Vintage Books, 1993), 17-31.

27 *Democracy in America,* 11.

28 Ibid., 336.

29 Ibid., volume II, chapter 2.

30 Walker Percy, *Love in the Ruins* (New York: Farrar Straus, & Giroux, 1971), 191.

31 Walter Gilbert, speech at a meeting of the Department of Energy, Santa Fe, 1986, quoted in *Forbidden Knowledge,* 178.

32 Descartes, *Discourse on Method,* part two, 11, trans. Donald Cress (Cambridge, Mass.: Hackett Publishing, 1980).

33 Descartes, *Meditations,* 1, trans. Donald Cress (Cambridge, Mass.: Hackett Publishing, 1994).

34 Hobbes, *Leviathan*, chapter 31, ed. Edwin Curley (Cambridge, Mass.: Hackett Publishing, 1994).

35 See William Paul, *Laughing Screaming* (New York: Columbia University Press, 1994), 409-30.

36 See Wes Gehring, *American Dark Comedy* (Westport, Ct.: Greenwood Press, 1996).

2 The Quest for Evil

1 Walker Percy, *Lancelot* (New York: Avon Books, 1977), 53-54.

2 *Beyond Good and Evil*, #44.

3 *Genealogy of Morals*, III, trans. F. Golffing (Garden City, NJ: Doubleday, 1956), 1.

4 Mark Edmundson, *Nightmare on Main Street: Angels, Sadomasochism, and the Culture of the Gothic* (Cambridge, Mass.: Harvard University Press, 1997), 16.

3 The Banality of Evil

1 Hannah Arendt, *Eichmann in Jerusalem: A Report on the Banality of Evil* (New York: Viking Press, 1965).

2 "Eichmann in Jerusalem: An Exchange of Letters Between Gershom Scholem and Hannah Arendt," in R. H. Fieldman, ed., *The Jew as Pariah*, (New York: Grove Press, 1978), 250-51.

3 L. Kohler and H. Saner, eds., *The Arendt-Jaspers Correspondence, 1926-1969* (New York: Harcourt Brace Jovanovich, 1992), 54, 62.

4 R.D.S. Jack, *Patterns of Divine Comedy*, (Suffolk: St. Edmundsbury Press, 1989), 12.

5 Roger Shattuck, "When Evil is 'Cool'," *The Atlantic Monthly*, January 1999, 73-78.

4 Normal Nihilism

1 Steve Pond, "Jerry Takes Shelter," *TV Guide*, February 4, 1995, 14.

2 Gavin Smith, "Quentin Tarantino," *Film Comment*, July/August 1994, 34.

3 Benjamin Svetkey, "Everything You Love or Hate About *Ally McBeal*," *Entertainment Weekly*, 30 January 1998, 24

4 Geoffrey O'Brien, "Sein of the Times," *New York Review of Books*, 14 August 1997.

5 "Everything You Love or Hate About *Ally McBeal*," *Entertainment Weekly*, January 30, 1998, 26

6 Ibid.

7 "Sein of the Times."

CONCLUSION: CHILDREN OF A LESSER GOD

1 *The Plain Sense of Things: The Fate of Religion in an Age of Normal Nihilism* (University Park, Penn.: Pennsylvania State University Press, 1997), 46.

2 Ibid., 52.

3 Ibid., 227-38.

4 *Love in the Ruins*, 3.

5 *Nightmare on Main Street*, 61-67.

6 Ibid., 178.

7 David Hume, *Dialogues Concerning Natural Religion* in *Classics of Western Philosophy*, 4th ed. by Steven M. Cahn, (Indianapolis: Hackett Press, 1997), 942.

8 Adrienne L. McLean, "Media Effects: Marshall McLuhan, Television Culture, and 'The X-Files'," *Film Quarterly* 51 (Summer 1998): 2-9.

Index

A NOTE ON THE AUTHOR

THOMAS S. HIBBS is associate professor of philosophy at Boston College. He has published two scholarly books on St. Thomas Aquinas and numerous essays on medieval philosophy, contemporary ethics, and popular culture. He earned his bachelor's and master's degrees at the University of Dallas and his doctorate at Notre Dame. He lives in Hudson, Massachusetts.

This book was designed and set into type
by Mitchell S. Muncy,
with cover art by Lee Whitmarsh,
and printed and bound
by Edwards Brothers, Inc.,
Ann Arbor, Michigan.

❦

The text face is Caslon,
designed by Carol Twombly,
based on faces cut by William Caslon, London, in the 1730s
and issued in digital form by Adobe Systems,
Mountain View, California, in 1989.

❦

The paper is acid-free and is of archival quality.

21